Also by the Author

THE WAY WE LIVED
A Photographic Record of Work in a Vanished America

THE STORY OF AMERICAN PHOTOGRAPHY

Detroit Publishing Company
Mobile, Alabama
1906

THE STORY OF AMERICAN PHOTOGRAPHY

An Illustrated History for Young People

MARTIN W. SANDLER

Little, Brown and Company

BOSTON   TORONTO

FIRST EDITION

The author wishes to thank the following persons, who have acted in an advisory capacity in the preparation of this book:

Lawrence Fink, chairman, Department of Education and Child Study, Smith College; Daniel Jones, photoarchivist, Peabody Museum, Harvard University; Joan Patterson Kerr, contributing editor, *American Heritage* magazine; Thomas Maloney, founder and publisher, *U.S. Camera;* Benjamin Michalski, president, American Society of Picture Professionals; John Wilmerding, assistant director, National Gallery of Art.

Library of Congress Cataloging in Publication Data

Sandler, Martin W.
  The story of American photography.

  Bibliography: p.
  Includes index.
  SUMMARY: Traces the development of photography in the United States. Illustrated with over 200 photographs.
  1. Photography—United States—History—Juvenile literature. [1. Photography—History] I. Title.
TR23.S34   770'.973   78-24025
ISBN 0-316-77021-3

*Published simultaneously in Canada
by Little, Brown & Company (Canada) Limited*

Contents

Unknown photographer
Photographing New York City
Stereograph
1905

Timothy O'Sullivan
Photographing the West
Wet-plate photograph
c. 1870

Preface

SINCE ITS INVENTION, photography has been the world's most popular picture-making process. At the same time, it has been the subject of questions as to whether or not it is a true art form. In our lifetime these questions have been answered with a resounding yes. The growth and appreciation of photography in the last two decades has been nothing short of phenomenal. Photography has taught us new ways of looking at the world. It has reshaped our entire visual experience.

The prominence of photography today can be seen in the ever-increasing number of photographic exhibitions in museums and galleries, in the proliferation of photographic books, in the meteoric rise in the number of students studying photography in high schools and colleges. Yet there has never been a history of photography prepared especially for young people.

That is the purpose of this book—to present to young people

Unknown photographer
Aerial Photographer
Dry-plate photograph
c. 1910

Unknown photographer
Photographing the West Coast
Stereograph
c. 1880

the detailed story of the growth of American photography. We have concentrated on American photography for several reasons. First, it is impossible within the pages of any one volume to deal with all of the cameramen and -women who have contributed to this important story; indeed, no one volume can cover all of the Americans who have made photography what it is today. Second, from the earliest daguerreotypists to the inventors of cameras that produce not only an image but a finished print, Americans have been at the forefront of every aspect of the story of photography.

In telling this story, an attempt has been made to bring to light the experiences, the frustrations, the successes of the established masters of American photography. But there is another important feature of this book as well. Through the years there have been scores of cameramen and -women whose remarkable talent has received little or no attention. The images taken by many of these artists have but recently been discovered. Throughout the pages of this book there are examples of the work of many hitherto little-known or completely unknown photographers whose work can stand proudly with that of the established masters.

At the back of this volume is a list of suggested readings. Those who wish to delve more deeply into the work of particular photographers or into specific aspects of photography will, it is hoped, find here a helpful guide. The story of American photography is a saga filled with drama and suspense, daring and achievement. How incredible that it is a story that is still less than one hundred fifty years old.

THE STORY OF AMERICAN PHOTOGRAPHY

Unknown photographer
Boy with Drum
Daguerreotype with case
c. 1845

One

The Beginnings
of Photography

VERY FEW INVENTIONS are the result of the work of one person. Although one man or woman may get credit for the "discovery," most inventions, like the automobile, the airplane, or the electric light, are the result of a number of people working independently toward the same goal. Each of these people contributes something that makes the final invention possible. Then, as often happens, one person puts all the pieces of the puzzle together, makes the "discovery" known, and receives credit for the invention.

Such was the case with the discovery of photography. The announcement of this astounding process was made to the world in 1839 by a Frenchman named Louis Jacques Mandé Daguerre. He, like many others, had been attempting for years to capture a permanent photographic image. His announcement, and the proof he offered that he had succeeded, brought him fame and wealth.

It also gave him the honor of having his name associated with the world's first form of photography—the *daguerreotype*.

Actually, Daguerre did not take the first photograph. Another Frenchman, named Joseph Nicéphore Niepce, had accomplished this some seventeen years before Daguerre made his announcement. And four years before Daguerre offered proof of his success, an Englishman, William Henry Fox Talbot, had taken a photograph on a one-inch-square paper negative.

Photography is based on two vital elements, one chemical, the other optical. Both of these elements have been known for hundreds of years. For example, in 1725 Johann Heinrich Schulze, a German scientist, discovered that light darkened silver salts. Schulze did not know it, but this was the basic chemical reaction upon which all of photography was to depend. What was needed was a way to make the image permanent, once light had formed it.

The optical element needed in making photography possible actually has been known for thousands of years. Aristotle was aware of it. Artists as early as the days of the Renaissance used the *camera obscura* as a means of holding an image long enough for it to be traced on paper. The first camera obscuras (darkrooms) were actually big enough for a person to stand inside. Light entered the darkened room through a small hole and projected on the opposite wall an inverted image of whatever lay outside. As years went on, the camera obscura was perfected in many ways. It was made smaller, and portable. Eventually, a lens was put into one end of the box, and ground glass was inserted flush with the top. A mirror was placed inside at a forty-five-degree

Early nineteenth-century camera obscura

angle. Thus, the projected image was now no longer upside-down and an artist could trace it by putting a thin sheet of paper over the glass.

The first person to recognize the connection between the optical and the chemical elements necessary in photography was an Englishman named Thomas Wedgwood. His goal was to use the camera obscura, not to trace images, but to capture a permanent picture on a metal plate. As early as 1799 he experimented with chemicals that he hoped would make this possible. However, the silver nitrate solution he used was not sensitive enough to produce a visible picture. Wedgwood's partner, Humphry Davy, continued the experiments, using silver chloride, which was more sensitive to light.

Neither Wedgwood nor Davy was able to produce an image with a camera, but they both succeeded in obtaining impressions of small objects, which they placed on their materials in direct sunlight. Even these images, however, darkened into obscurity once the objects were removed, and both Wedgwood and Davy died without achieving their goal. Attempts at obtaining a permanent image continued, and by 1826 Joseph Nicéphore Niepce had succeeded in combining chemicals in such a way as to make the securing of a faint positive permanent image possible. Niepce was one step away from obtaining the sharp permanent image that many had sought. But he was in poor health and out of money. In 1829 he entered into a partnership with Louis Daguerre. According to the terms of the partnership, Niepce was to contribute his knowledge of making silver, copper, or glass plates. Daguerre was to contribute his "new adaptation of the camera obscura."

Daguerre journeyed to Niepce's home, where Niepce demonstrated his techniques to him in detail. They then went their separate ways to work toward perfecting the invention. They were never to meet again. In 1833 Niepce died, and Daguerre continued his experiments on his own.

It was Daguerre, using a chemical that neither Niepce nor Wedgwood nor Davy had tried, who found the missing link. The ingredient Daguerre hit upon was mercury. After eleven years of experimenting, Daguerre found that by letting mercury vapors develop the image, he could produce a photographic plate that was permanent and sharper than any that had been made before.

Daguerre's achievement was publicly announced on August 19, 1839. The daguerreotype, a silver-coated copper sheet made sensitive to light, exposed in a camera, and developed by mercury vapors, was an individual picture. It was not a negative. It could be seen only when held at the proper angle, away from direct light. As a one-of-a-kind positive image, it could not be reproduced or printed in large numbers. This feat would not be achieved until the negative-positive process became perfected.

Still, with the daguerrotype the age of photography had begun. And it caused a sensation! Never before had it been possible to record things exactly as they were. Images of homes, businesses—landmarks of all kinds—could be captured and they would be, in the words of early daguerreotypists, "positively true to nature." Most important, human likenesses could be recorded. Unlike those drawn by artists, the new photographic portraits were exact replicas of the subject. And for the first time, people from all walks of life could have their pictures recorded for posterity. Before photography the only way a person could have his or her likeness captured was to commission an artist to draw it. This was very expensive and only the wealthy could afford it. Now with the relatively inexpensive daguerreotype process, anyone could have a portrait to display proudly in living room or office. It would be a picture that would remain long after the subject had passed away, reminding future generations of the person and showing clearly what he or she looked like.

Hundreds of thousands of people sat before the daguerreotype camera—despite the fact that from the beginning the experience was a true ordeal. At first a person had to sit for almost twenty minutes in the full sun in order to have a daguerreotype taken. The earliest daguerreotype subjects actually got sunburned while enduring the long exposure. Within a year, however, the process

Unknown photographer
Early Daguerreotypist at Work
c. 1850

had been improved and the exposure time was reduced to two minutes. Eventually this was reduced further to thirty seconds. Even a half minute was torture, however, when one considers that the subject could not move a muscle during the picture taking or the picture would be ruined. Neck clamps were often used to help people keep perfectly still. No wonder our ancestors look so grim in the daguerreotypes that have been passed down through the years.

Still, despite the torturous process, the known and the unknown poured into the photographers' studios. Thanks to the daguerreotype we can see what important figures like John Quincy Adams, Zachary Taylor, and Washington Irving looked like. Scholars use

Unknown photographer
Zachary Taylor
Daguerreotype
c. 1845

the early 1840s as a historical benchmark. If someone lived before that date, no one can tell exactly what the person looked like. If, on the other hand, a well-known figure lived after 1840, then the chances are great that there is a photograph of that person and his or her exact features are there for all to see.

The daguerreotype process could not capture motion. All daguerreotypes, however, were not portraits. Many daguerreotypists did leave their studios to capture scenes that show us what different locales looked like in the years immediately following the birth of photography. Sometimes, if they were lucky or skilled enough, they were able to train their cameras on a group of people for a long enough time before anyone moved to obtain a shot of people in natural surroundings. One cameraman, for example, produced an early photograph of eight gentlemen enjoying the view at Niagara Falls. Another was able to record a military muster on the Common in Boston. Other early photographers were able to capture similar interesting scenes with daguerreotype cameras.

Nowhere was the daguerreotype adopted more quickly than in the United States. The most famous pioneer American daguerreotypist was Samuel F. B. Morse. A well-known portrait painter, a professor at New York University, and the inventor of the telegraph, Morse had traveled to Paris in 1839 to see Daguerre at work. He and his partner, John W. Draper, took many daguerreotypes of their own, but Morse's main contribution to photography was as a teacher of the daguerreotype method. Among his students were Edward Anthony, Albert Southworth, and the most famous of all early American photographers, Mathew B. Brady.

Mathew B. Brady
Washington Irving
Daguerreotype
c. 1852

Unknown photographer
Group at Niagara Falls
Daguerreotype
c. 1845

Southworth and Hawes
Muster on Boston Common
Daguerreotype
c. 1845

12

Unknown photographer
Family Group
Daguerreotype
1854

American inventiveness quickly brought many improvements to the daguerreotype. Smaller cameras were perfected, better lenses were invented, and the length of exposure time was even further reduced. Daguerreotype portrait studios sprang up across the United States. By 1855 there were more than ninety galleries in New York City alone. Every American city and most large towns had several daguerreotype galleries.

Daguerreotyping required little monetary investment and the skills needed to do it could be learned with reasonable effort. Daguerreotypes were so much in demand that many shopkeepers, doctors, and craftsmen of all kinds opened daguerreotype galleries as a sideline. Often the quality of their work was poor by any standards.

There were daguerreotypists, however, who built solid reputations as true artists. John Plumbe, Jr., for example, was the owner of a chain of fourteen daguerreotype studios in eastern and midwestern cities. He hired and trained his cameramen carefully, and his work was of the highest quality. Plumbe was one of those early daguerreotypists who ventured outside the portrait studio. In recent years an important discovery of some of his earliest daguerreotypes was made. Included in the find was a series of the earliest architectural photographs ever taken of this nation's capital. Made around the year 1846, these Plumbe daguerreotypes show us what the White House (then called the President's House), the Capitol Building, the Patent Office, and other government buildings looked like when James K. Polk was President of the United States.

John Plumbe, Jr.
The President's House
Daguerreotype
c. 1845

Albert Southworth and Josiah Hawes of Boston were two other exceptional daguerreotypists. They produced striking photographs of the leading personalities and landmarks of that city. Their work was marked by careful attention to detail and their daguerreotypes are today regarded as some of the finest examples of the art. The same can be said of Edward Anthony and his partner, J. M. Edwards, who operated out of Washington, D.C. They photographed every leading political figure of the day and formed the National Daguerrean Gallery, which was on exhibition in New York City.

As noted, not all of these early photographers confined themselves to their studios. Perhaps the greatest of the outdoor daguerreotypists was Alexander Hesler. He took marvelous daguerreotypes of the frontier areas on the upper Mississippi and in Minnesota Territory. One of his daguerreotypes of the Minnehaha Falls in that region came into the hands of the American poet Henry Wadsworth Longfellow. Hesler achieved instant fame when Longfellow credited the photograph as having served as the inspiration for his classic *Song of Hiawatha*.

By far the most famous and most successful of all American daguerreotypists was Mathew B. Brady. His studios in New York and Washington were the most famous, elegant, and successful anywhere. All the greats and near-greats of the era stopped at one time or another for their "Photograph by Brady." Brady became as important for his organizational skills as for his ability as a cameraman. He was able to put together teams of photographers for special projects. This ability became particularly important in the 1860s when the Civil War erupted.

As is the case with all forms of early photography, discoveries are continually being made of important early daguerreotypes. Perhaps the most spectacular "find" to date took place in 1977 at the Peabody Museum at Harvard University when a group of daguerreotypes showing American slaves was uncovered. Accompanying documents revealed that these daguerreotypes were taken on a Columbia, South Carolina, plantation in 1850 by a photographer named J. T. Zealy.

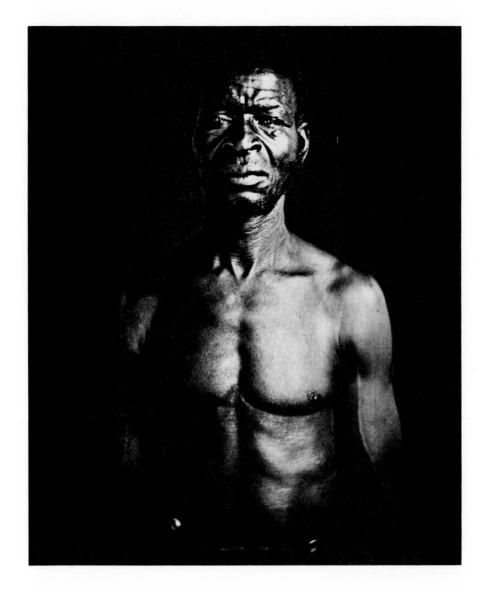

J. T. Zealy
Jack, a Slave
Daguerreotype
1850

Despite its tremendous popularity, the era of the daguerreotype lasted only about a dozen years. Fierce competition drove prices down to a point where daguerreotypists could not make a profit. In the beginning of the 1840s the average price for a daguerreotype with its case was two dollars. By the end of the 1840s there were studios turning out portraits at two for twenty-five cents.

The fact that the daguerreotype was hard to look at because of its metallic glare and could not be easily duplicated added to its demise. By the 1850s new methods of photography were being perfected that would replace the daguerreotype completely. Still, its place in history was assured — for the daguerreotype was indeed the first real form of photography.

Just three weeks after Louis Daguerre made his historic announcement, the Englishman William Henry Fox Talbot reported that he had succeeded in capturing permanent images on paper. After many experiments, Talbot produced what was called the *calotype,* or sometimes *Talbotype.* It was a paper negative from which limitless prints could be made. The images produced by the calotype were not as clear as those of the daguerreotype, but many people found appeal in their soft tones. Like the daguerreotype, the calotype had a short-lived history. It became obsolete when, in 1851, an important new photographic process was announced. Like the daguerreotype, however, it too played a vital role in photographic history, for the negative-positive process it introduced formed the basis for all modern photography.

In 1851 another Englishman, Frederick Scott Archer, originated the *collodion* process of making negatives on glass. This was

W. and F. Langenheim
Views in North America
Talbotypes
1850

19

a great improvement over both metal and paper negatives. The collodion process was easier to work with than the daguerreotype and it was much more sensitive than the calotype. It provided a negative image on glass from which an unlimited number of prints of the highest quality could be made. There are many photographic historians today who believe that the finest images ever taken were produced by the collodion process.

Collodion was a gluey liquid that was spread on glass plates and coated with light-sensitive chemicals. The plates had to be exposed while moist and developed immediately, because the coating's sensitivity to light diminished as it dried. This was therefore called the "wet-plate process."

Photographers everywhere began to use the wet plate. It was the standard negative material from 1855 until the invention of the dry plate in 1880. With the perfection of this process, an increasing number of amateurs became attracted to photography. Slowly but surely, photography was becoming an American folk art—the most democratic art the world has ever known.

The collodion process was used in a variety of ways. For example, when a wet plate was put on a black cloth, the captured image appeared as a positive. It could then be placed inside an ornate case and displayed in the family parlor. These collodion positives were called *ambrotypes*.

Another kind of collodion process was the tremendously popular *tintype*. To produce a tintype, collodion was poured over a piece of metal that had been coated with a dark varnish. Tintypes were stronger than glass and very inexpensive to produce. Even

Timothy O'Sullivan
Black Cañon from Mirror Bar
Wet-plate photograph
c. 1870

Unknown photographer
Union Naval Officers Aboard Civil War Vessel
Wet-plate photograph
1863

Unknown photographer
New York Harbor
Wet-plate photograph
c. 1870

Unknown photographer
Young Man with Hat
Tintype
c. 1875

24

though they had almost no artistic value, they became immensely popular in the United States. Traveling tintype "professors" sprang up across the nation. They and their cameras could be seen at carnivals, beaches, and on boardwalks everywhere. Hundreds of thousands of tintypes were sold in America. They were even used in rings, tiepins, and cuff links. Some of the nation's finest photographers began their careers by taking and selling tintypes. Frances Benjamin Johnston, for example, had a highly successful tintype business before she set it aside to become one of America's best-known documentary photographers.

It was still another form of the collodion process, however, that was to become the most popular of all. In 1854 a Frenchman named Adolphe Eugène Disdéri patented the *carte de visite,* a name he gave to both the camera he invented and the photographs it took. The *carte de visite* camera had several lenses and a photo holder that moved. As many as twelve portraits could be taken on one wet-plate negative. The paper print from the negative could then be cut up into individual prints. These were pasted on 4-by-2½-inch mounts and used much as business cards are used today.

The *carte de visite* revolutionized photography. Hundreds of thousands of people had their pictures taken and left their photographic cards wherever they went to visit. Mothers regularly brought their children to *carte de visite* studios to have their growth recorded for relatives and friends. It became a common practice in America to exchange *cartes de visite* at holidays or birthdays. As people acquired more and more of the photographic

Frances Benjamin Johnston
Tintype Studio
c. 1890

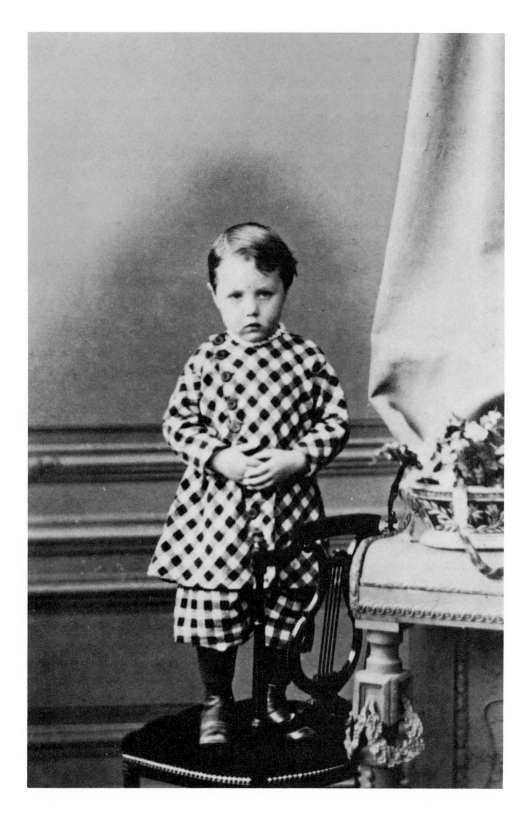

Unknown photographer
Carte de visite
c. 1860

Unknown photographer
Carte de visite
c. 1860

Unknown photographers
Cartes de visite
c. 1860

cards, a way was needed to preserve and present them. Thus was born the *carte de visite* album. Many of these were very elaborate, bound in beautiful and expensive leather. In the late nineteenth century the *carte de visite* album, along with the stereograph viewer and album, which were soon to join it, could be found in American parlors all across the country.

By 1870 photography had become so popular that there were more than three hundred photographic galleries in New York City alone. These studios were doing a booming business, not only in *cartes de visite*, but in another collodion-process-inspired type of photography as well. These were the cabinet-size—4-by-5½-inch—portraits of the nation's leading theatrical personalities, dressed in the costumes of their best-known roles.

In an age before radio, television, or mass sports, theatrical personalities were among the leading heroes and heroines of the nation. Studios were able to sell thousands of these cabinet-size photographs of such stage performers as Joseph Jefferson, Lillian Russell, and Mary Anderson. The most famous and successful of all of these theatrical photographers was Napoleon Sarony. Every leading actor and actress posed for him in his New York studio. Sarony had a warm and enthusiastic personality, which put his subjects at ease and allowed him to capture them in poses that were relaxed and natural. He was a showman himself, and every photograph he sold carried his flowery signature printed in bright red ink across the bottom. Most important, he was a highly talented cameraman, who produced many photographs that were artistic as well as popular.

Napoleon Sarony
Mary Anderson As Galatea
Theatrical card
1883

Miss ANDERSON as GALATEA.
Copyright 1883, by Napoleon Sarony.

NEW YORK

31

The invention of the collodion process made possible still another important and tremendously popular photographic form—the *stereograph*. The principle of the stereograph had actually been put forth by a man named Charles Wheatstone as early as 1838. This principle lies in the fact that a person's two eyes see slightly different images when directed at a given object. The two images are combined in the brain to produce the sensation of depth or perspective. Wheatstone believed that if two perspective drawings were made that reproduced exactly the image seen by each eye, then depth perception would be re-created. Attempts were made to draw pairs of pictures so exactly that this three-dimensional effect could be achieved. This was such exacting and difficult work, however, that it proved impractical.

But, with the coming of the camera and the collodion wet-plate process, this could now be done. A special stereographic camera was devised that used two lenses placed two and a half inches apart. This is the average distance between the human eyes. Each lens recorded the image seen by one eye, and when the finished stereographic print was placed in a viewer called a *stereoscope,* a three-dimensional effect was achieved.

Photographers throughout the United States turned their attention to the stereograph. Millions of views were taken of all parts of the nation. Some of the earliest frontier photographers used stereographic equipment. Scenes of crowded cities, booming mining towns, and exotic places around the globe were taken and turned into stereographs. Americans could sit comfortably in their parlors or drawing rooms and, through their stereoscopes, see Chinese laborers posed by huge locomotive-driven snowplows as they

Unknown photographer
Railroad Snowplow
Full stereograph
c. 1870

Unknown photographer
Yosemite Valley
One half of stereograph
c. 1885

33

cleared the way for the transcontinental railroad. They could see spectacular scenes of wilderness areas in the West that few people had ever visited. City dwellers could view authentic Indians of the Great Plains, mounted on horseback ready for attack. Stereoscope owners from rural areas all over America could get a first-hand glimpse of Wall Street, the nation's financial capital. No place seemed too remote for the photographer and his stereo camera. In an age before movies, radio, or television, enterprising photographers created a whole series of humorous stereographs designed to turn the living room, with its viewer and album, into an entertainment center.

Stereographs became so immensely popular that large companies were formed dealing exclusively with this new form of photography. Companies such as E. & H. T. Anthony, Keystone, and Underwood and Underwood helped feed the public's seemingly never satisfied appetite for more and more stereographic views. The single most important champion of the stereograph in America was the famous writer Oliver Wendell Holmes, who boasted that he had viewed more than one hundred thousand stereographs. Holmes was so taken with the potential of the stereograph as a means of recording history that he recommended the establishment of national and city stereographic libraries.

His recommendation was never carried out, but what Holmes was able to see was that in the long run stereographic views would have far more importance than that of merely presenting pictures in three dimensions. They would provide us with a marvelously documented record of people and places in a society that has all but vanished.

Unknown photographer
Wall Street, New York
One half of stereograph
c. 1900

Unknown photographer
Plains Indians
One half of stereograph
c. 1885

Unknown photographer
The Smoker
One half of stereograph
c. 1885

Two

The Mirror with a Memory

T HE MIRROR WITH A MEMORY" is what Oliver Wendell Holmes called the camera. By the 1860s, less than twenty-five years after Louis Daguerre's historic announcement, this mirror with a memory was already becoming an important part of American life. The introduction of the wet plate opened up whole new worlds to photographers, and studios continued to spring up throughout the nation. Events were soon to take place that would gain photography even more recognition and make it more important than ever before. The American Civil War and, following that conflict, the beginning of official surveys of the American West would soon take cameramen far away from the comfort of their studios.

Photographing the Civil War

In the middle of the 1880s one person, more than any other, dominated the field of American photography. His name was Mathew B. Brady, and he was destined to become even more important and to rank with the most famous photographers of all time. Brady was one of a number of young photographers who received their training from Samuel F. B. Morse. He was a tireless worker who not only displayed a fine talent for taking photographs but also possessed a real business sense. In 1844, at the age of twenty-one, he opened his first daguerreotype studio in New York. In that same year he was awarded first prize at the American Institute in New York for one of his daguerreotypes. It was the first of many gold medals and other awards he would win for his photography.

Brady's gallery was a tremendous success from the very beginning. The most famous people of his time came to his studio to be photographed. Among his early subjects were such celebrities as Daniel Webster, John Quincy Adams, and an aged Andrew Jackson. Brady's New York studio was so successful that in 1849 he opened another studio in Washington. This put him into even closer contact with the most important political figures of the day.

Brady was always searching for innovations in photography. He was, for example, one of the first to perfect a method of hand-coloring daguerreotypes. He spent years working on a publication he entitled *The Gallery of Illustrious Americans,* which included photographs and biographical sketches of leading personalities and was one of the first photographic books ever published.

Brady's business continued to grow to such an extent that by 1860 he had opened two new galleries in New York. Each was more elaborate than the previous one. In 1860 in his National Portrait Gallery in New York Brady took his most famous portrait. In the midst of the Lincoln-Douglas political debates, Abraham Lincoln arrived for a speech at the Cooper Union, a college in New York City. Accompanied by three members of the Young Men's Republican Committee, the candidate from Illinois went to Brady's gallery and had his portrait taken. After the important speech at the Cooper Union the next day, Brady's Lincoln portrait was in great demand. Thousands were sold and woodcuts were made from them for use in the leading news publications of the day. After Lincoln was elected President, he went to Brady's Washington studio for an inauguration portrait. While there, he stated, "Brady and the Cooper Union speech made me President."

Not long after Lincoln's inauguration, events took place that dramatically changed the course of the nation's history and the career of Mathew Brady. By 1861, the rift between North and South became irreconcilable, and in April of that year the Civil War began. By this time Brady, like most American photographers, had abandoned the daguerreotype and was working exclusively with wet plates. He was convinced that he could organize teams of photographers, provide them with photographic wagons that could both carry the equipment they needed and serve as darkrooms in which to develop the wet plates, and take himself and his teams onto the battlefields.

Brady had many influential friends on both sides of the conflict.

Mathew B. Brady
Cooper Union Lincoln Portrait
1860

He used these contacts to gain the necessary permission to accompany the Union Army into the field. He was not concerned with the politics of the war. Brady's purpose was simple and clear — he was determined to become America's first battlefield photographer, the cameraman of the Civil War.

Between the time that war was declared and the first actual battle, Washington was a beehive of activity. Supplies were being gathered, troops were being trained, military strategy was being planned. Meanwhile, Brady's studio there was busier than ever before as thousands of soldiers made their way up its stairs to have *cartes de visite* of themselves in uniform taken to be sent to loved ones at home. These photographs are important today for they reveal, among other things, the incredible youth of many soldiers in both armies. For Brady, this was a time in which all the logistics of putting teams of photographers into the field had to be completed. From January to April of 1862 he hired and trained the men who were to become America's first war photographers. Brady assigned these men to different territories in the war zones and arranged for the setting up of photographic bases in those areas.

There has always been controversy as to just how many of the dramatic Civil War photographs were taken by Brady himself. We know, for example, that Timothy O'Sullivan actually snapped the greatest number of pictures. Alexander Gardner took many others. We also know, however, that hundreds of the photographs *were* taken by Brady and that he was present at some of the most important battles of the war, coming close to injury or death on

Mathew B. Brady
Union Army Private
Carte de visite
c. 1861

Mathew B. Brady
Confederate Army Private
Carte de visite
c. 1861

several occasions. In fact, he received his baptism under fire at the very first major engagement of the conflict—the Battle of Bull Run.

Brady and his companions had two photographic wagons at Bull Run. They were specially designed to serve as darkrooms and had built-in shelves to hold chemicals, glass negatives, cameras, and other equipment. These photographic wagons soon became familiar sights at camps and battlefields throughout the war

Unknown photographer
"Whatsit Wagon"
1861

zones. The soldiers gave the wagons a name. "It's the Whatsit," they would shout whenever Brady or one of his fellow photographers arrived on the scene. Actually the "Whatsits" proved to be excellent targets for artillery blasts, and on more than one occasion Brady or one of the other members of the photographic team was lucky to escape with his life as shells exploded all around the wagon.

When the Battle of Bull Run began, Brady and his team of photographers immediately set up their cameras. There they took the first photographs of an American battlefield on the same day as the battle. The cameras of the time still did not allow for the capturing of action shots. But as soon as the firing stopped the photographers were on the field, recording dramatic images of the dead, the wounded — all the remnants of the historic skirmish.

The Battle of Bull Run was a disaster for the Union Army. Before it was over, most of the troops had turned and fled. Since the battle was fought close to Washington, Brady decided to return there with his wagon before setting out for the next theater of operation. Only a few hours after his return to the capital, word leaked out about the photographs he had taken. One newspaper proclaimed, "The public is indebted to Brady . . . for his excellent views of grim-visaged war. He has been in Virginia with his camera and many and spirited are the pictures he has taken. His are the only records of the flight of Bull Run."

The Battle of Bull Run marked the beginning of American military photography. Throughout the rest of the war Brady, O'Sullivan, Gardner, and the other members of the photographic teams

Mathew B. Brady
1st Connecticut Artillery
1862

Mathew B. Brady
Confederate Dead
1862

A. J. Russell
Aftermath of Battle
1863

took picture after picture of every aspect of the war—soldiers in camp awaiting battle, scenes at the battlefield moments after the firing had stopped, military hospitals and prisons, generals and privates, victors and vanquished. They risked the constant dangers of battle and worked under the most difficult conditions— freezing cold in the winters of 1862 and 1863 and burning heat in the summer of 1864.

By the middle of the war, Brady had more than thirty bases of operation. The photographs that were sent back to the Washington studio from the front had a tremendous impact upon the American public. Said one newspaper, "Mr. Brady has done something to bring home to us the terrible reality and earnestness of war. . . . Crowds of people are constantly going up the stairs [of his studio]. Follow them and you will find them bending over photographic views of the fearful battlefield, taken immediately after the action."

Brady, O'Sullivan, and the other combat photographers captured images of every phase of the conflict. Not only were photographs taken on land, but for the first time in American history, pictures of a navy at war were taken as well. During the early stages of the conflict, there were rather lengthy periods of quiet between battles. The war photographers used this time to take hundreds of pictures of soldiers and their officers in camp. The cameramen obviously were able to compose these camp pictures more carefully than their battlefield shots, and many of the photographs that resulted were truly outstanding. A photograph taken by Brady, for example, of three Union officers leaning

Mathew B. Brady
Union Gunners Aboard Ship
1863

Mathew B. Brady
Officers of 1st Connecticut Artillery
1863

50

Alexander Gardner
Lincoln at Antietam
1862

against a tree reveals the photographer's expertise at composition and his sense of the dramatic (page 51).

A sense of the dramatic is also present in Alexander Gardner's photograph of President Abraham Lincoln visiting with General George McClellan and his staff at their field headquarters at Antietam in 1862. Lincoln, stovepipe hat and all, has been placed in the center of the photograph. The officers are posed facing him, all eyes supposedly riveted on the commander in chief. But as so often happened, the lure of the camera was too much for some of the men, and even in the presence of the President, they turned and stared into the lens.

Later in the war, during another lull between battles, Timothy O'Sullivan took an important sequence of photographs. From a church window nearby, he captured three successive scenes of General Ulysses S. Grant at a strategy session with some of his officers (pages 54–55). The three photographs viewed together give one the sense of movement. O'Sullivan thus became one of the first photographers to hint at the possibilities of motion caught by the lens of a camera.

In January of 1863 Alexander Gardner left Brady's employ to go into business for himself. He was hired by the Union Army Secret Service as its official photographer. Gardner's chief job was to take pictures of groups of soldiers so that the Secret Service could study them to see if any known Confederate spies had made their way into the Union ranks. On his own Gardner took many photographs of every aspect of the war. Some of his photographs are now acclaimed as being among the most dramatic Civil War

Timothy O'Sullivan
General Grant with Officers
1864

views of all. They include many scenes of areas in the South that lay in ruins after the Union Army had passed through them.

By 1864 it was obvious that the valor and dedication of the Confederate troops were in the end no match for the immense superiority of manpower and supplies held by the Union Army. When word came in the spring of 1865 of General Robert E. Lee's willingness to surrender, Brady was taking photographs of the last military engagements in the North. He rushed to Appomattox, Virginia, where the official surrender took place, but was too late to capture the scene. He then hurried to Richmond, where he knew Lee had gone. It was while en route to Richmond that he received the tragic news of the assassination of President Lincoln. Brady arrived at the Lee home in Richmond and, after several attempts, received permission to photograph the gallant Confederate general. Lee posed for Brady in the uniform he had worn at the surrender. The photograph was an important one, because the general had not had any photograph of himself taken during the conflict. Brady's picture, which was widely circulated, gave the nation its first real look at the brilliant Southern commander.

With the end of the war, thousands of soldiers poured through the streets of Washington on their way home. Many stopped to have *cartes de visite* taken at Brady's studio. Often they were the same soldiers who had posed in the days just prior to their leaving for the battlefield. The contrast between how they looked at war's end and how they had looked some four years before provided a grim commentary on the tragic toll that the war had taken on even those who had survived.

Alexander Gardner
Ruins of Charleston, South Carolina
1865

Mathew B. Brady
Robert E. Lee
1865

Once the war was over, Brady ran into serious financial difficulties. He had expected that his war views would be sold in such quantities that they would cover the huge costs he took on in setting up his operation. Such was not the case. His main hope was that the government would pay him a good sum for his collection. This did not happen either. Then, while crossing a Washington street, he was struck by a horse-drawn streetcar. He suffered injuries that ended his photographic career. His financial situation became worse, and he was finally forced to accept aid from the military society to which he belonged. A major exhibition of his war photographs was planned, but on January 16, 1896, before the exhibition could be held, he died.

The career of the man who dominated the first fifty-seven years of American photography had ended. Like many other geniuses, he died in poverty. But as one historian has said, "As long as the medium of photography survives, so will the credit line 'Photograph by Brady' be remembered."

Photographing the West

Once the Civil War was over, a whole class of American photographers found themselves with unique training and experience but no employment. These were, of course, the men who, either as part of Mathew Brady's camera teams or on their own, had survived the rigors of combat photography and recorded the scenes of the Civil War on glass. They were used to working under the most difficult conditions, and they had experience in coping with all the problems of taking and developing wet plates in the field.

Many of these photographers put this experience to work by signing on as official photographers for the railroad companies, which, after the Civil War, were busily laying tracks in the frontier areas of the West. Others became part of the many geological survey teams financed by the United States government immediately following the war. These government expeditions were organized for various reasons. The purpose of some was simply to explore the wild, unsettled territories in the West. Others were formed to establish territorial boundaries in those areas. Still others were true geological surveys in that their main objective was to look for mineral deposits. Whatever their purpose, all of these expeditions hired official photographers to make a permanent record of lands that few Americans had seen. The photographs they took rank among the most spectacular landscape photographs ever taken.

Photography on the frontier actually began before the Civil War. There, daguerreotypists, most of whose names are lost to us forever, captured scenes of frontier towns, riverboats, miners, and Indian chiefs. One of these daguerreotypists whose work did survive was a Californian named Robert H. Vance. He took many views of the people, early towns, and rivers of California, as well as of Indian tribes located in that region. He was particularly interested in the men and women who poured into the goldfields of California after gold was discovered there in 1849. Vance traveled east in 1851, where an exhibition of some three hundred of his photographs was held in New York. The publicity he received from the exhibition helped establish his reputation as one of America's first frontier photographers.

The most famous, and without doubt the best, of all the photographers who captured views of the American West before the end of the Civil War was another Californian, Carleton E. Watkins. He had been trained by Vance, and early in his career he took many daguerreotypes of the California region. He switched to the wet-plate process, however, as soon as it was available, and by 1861 he was in the Yosemite Valley taking dramatic landscape views. These photographs are particularly important, because they represent the first series of pictures taken that showed the landscape as a total wilderness, before the arrival of man.

Watkins used two types of cameras in his work in the Yosemite Valley. One was a stereoscopic camera for taking the stereographic views that were so popular back east. The other was an enormous camera that he had specially made for him by a San Francisco cabinetmaker. It could hold huge glass plates, probably as large as seventeen by twenty-two inches, and enabled Watkins to capture spectacular views of the untouched wilderness. One can only imagine the difficulties he encountered as he hauled his enormous camera and the huge, fragile glass plates across gorges and up and down the sides of mountains. One contemporary photographer noted with amazement that Watkins "packed in his apparatus on mules and took a series of the finest photographs I have ever seen."

Watkins continued to photograph in the Yosemite Valley until 1867, when he returned to San Francisco and opened a gallery there. Although Watkins began his work before the era of the official railroad and government surveys, he did become involved in both types of expeditions. In 1870 he joined a geological expedition headed by Clarence King, a man who in his lifetime headed

Carleton E. Watkins
Yosemite
c. 1861

63

several such projects. In 1873 Watkins took photographs of the Central Pacific Railroad. In his later years he often hired himself out to landowners who paid him to take photographs of their farms and ranches. He took as much care in capturing these landscapes as he did with his Yosemite Valley pictures. As one historian has said, the photographs of Carleton E. Watkins show a person "in love with nature."

Another frontier photographer who began his work before the end of the Civil War was Eadweard J. Muybridge. In many ways his career paralleled that of Carleton Watkins. Both were lovers of nature, both spent a great deal of time taking photographs in the Yosemite Valley, and both also spent time recording scenes along the route of the Central Pacific Railroad. Eadweard Muybridge, however, was destined to win a unique place in the annals of the history of photography, an achievement that had nothing to do with the photography of the West, for it was Muybridge who later accomplished the long-awaited feat of capturing motion in still pictures. Yet, even if he had not made this noted contribution, Muybridge would still be remembered as one of America's earliest and most important landscape photographers. His spectacular photograph taken from Glacier Rock Number 36 at Yosemite Falls is a prime example of his talent with landscapes. A solitary seated figure in the center of the picture is dwarfed by a large tree in the foreground and the falls and the mountains in the distance. Dark shadows accent the foreground and form a dramatic contrast to the bright sunlight that dominates the rest of the photograph.

Of all the men who earned their living by making photographic records of the progress of the nation's transcontinental railroad, the two most famous were Alexander Gardner and A. J. Russell. Gardner, as noted earlier, was one of the most important Civil War photographers. After the war he went to Kansas, where he made a series of views along the Union Pacific Railroad. At the time that Gardner was in Kansas, the majority of the people there lived along the route of the railroad. Gardner took many stereoscopic views of the people, their towns, and their ways of life. The stereographs of this frontier and its people that he sent back east became extremely popular and gave people in the established communities their first look at those who had left to begin a new life on the frontier.

Captain A. J. Russell, another former Civil War cameraman, also made his mark as a railroad photographer. Russell was hired as official photographer for the Union Pacific Railroad. It was his job to record every aspect of the work as the railway slowly but surely made its way westward to link up with the Central Pacific Railroad line progressing from the West. Russell kept a journal of his experiences and this, along with the dramatic photographs he took, chronicles one of the most important developments in all of American history—the linking of East and West by rail. His photograph entitled "Valley of Bitter Creek" (page 68) is a marvelous visual documentation of the seemingly impassable terrain and the seemingly endless distances that had to be conquered by men such as those in the photograph, before the transcontinental railroad could be completed.

Alexander Gardner
Outside Lawrence, Kansas
1869

A. J. Russell
Valley of Bitter Creek
1869

Vance, Watkins, Muybridge, Gardner, Russell—they were all important photographers of the West. They took photographs that allowed Americans to view lands and people they would otherwise never have seen. Some of their photographs, particularly those of Watkins and Muybridge, are true works of art.

The two men, however, who earned the greatest reputation, and who captured perhaps the most spectacular western views of all, were Timothy H. O'Sullivan and William Henry Jackson. Timothy O'Sullivan was born in New York City. His parents were immigrants from Ireland. He was only sixteen or seventeen years old when he began serving as an apprentice to Mathew Brady. He was only twenty-one when he was taking pictures with Brady at the Battle of Bull Run. O'Sullivan serves as a perfect example of the importance of the expeditionary photographer in the history of American photography.

One of the first of the government-sponsored expeditions was the Fortieth Parallel Survey led by Clarence King in 1867. O'Sullivan was hired as the official photographer. The report of the survey stated, "The section to be surveyed is a belt of land about a hundred miles near the fortieth parallel of latitude, between the hundred twentieth and the hundred and fifth degrees of longitude or, in other words, from Virginia City (Nevada) to Denver City, a stretch of eight hundred or nine hundred miles in length. . . . It is the object of the Government to ascertain all the characteristics of the region. . . . The minerals, the flora and the fauna of the country are likewise to be studied and reported on. In fact, all the work of nature in that wild and unknown region is to be scanned by shrewd and highly-educated observers."

The King survey started out in July of 1867 and crossed the Sierra Nevada Mountains, coming upon the mining towns of western Nevada. There, at Virginia City, O'Sullivan descended deep into the mine known as the Comstock Lode to photograph the miners at work. He used a magnesium flash rig he had devised in order to capture his images in the dark caverns below the earth's surface.

The survey party then continued eastward down a number of dangerous rivers and across wasteland that few human beings had ever seen. By 1869 they had reached the Great Salt Lake basin. Using a mule-drawn ambulance to haul water for use in his traveling darkroom, O'Sullivan photographed the shifting sand dunes near Sand Springs, Nevada. One of his most dramatic photographs was of this solitary ambulance standing against the vast white expanse of the desert.

By October of 1868 the party was at the magnificent Shoshone Falls region on the Snake River. There, like Watkins before him, O'Sullivan hauled heavy cameras and equipment to the very top of the cliffs and captured spectacular views of the region.

In September of 1869 the King survey ended and O'Sullivan immediately signed on as the photographer to another expedition. This was the Davis survey, whose task it was to travel to Panama and determine possible routes for a canal through that country. O'Sullivan found the dense and dark jungle there much less appealing for his form of photography, and in 1871 this energetic and adventurous man was back in the West again, this time as photographer to an expedition under the command of Lieutenant

Timothy O'Sullivan
Sand Springs, Nevada
1867

Timothy O'Sullivan
Black Cañon of the Colorado
1871

72

Timothy O'Sullivan
Fortification Rock, Arizona
1871

Timothy O'Sullivan
Canyon de Chelly
1873

George M. Wheeler of the Army Corps of Engineers. The main purpose of this expedition was to explore the territories of Nevada, Utah, Arizona, and New Mexico. The terrain of this area provided O'Sullivan with a backdrop for some of his most interesting photographs. The views he took of the canyons in Arizona, for example, were extraordinary for the ways in which they combined the tones and textures of water, sand, rock, and the Arizona light.

Several of the views show the small boat O'Sullivan used to cross the lakes and rivers in the unspoiled region. The large black-draped box in the bow served as his darkroom for developing whatever wet plates he took while using the boat. While he was in the region, O'Sullivan also took some still lifes. His photograph of a bottle placed beside a rock carved by drifting sand reveals his true artistry and versatility with the camera (page 73).

In 1873 O'Sullivan led an expedition of his own into the Southwest, where he photographed the Zuñi and Magia pueblos and the Indians who still lived in that area. While there, he took what became perhaps his most famous photograph—that of the awesome abandoned cliff dwellings in that part of Arizona known as the Canyon de Chelly. This area contained Indian cliff dwellings that had been abandoned in the thirteenth century. O'Sullivan took full advantage of the play of light against wind- and sand-chiseled sides of the cliffs to produce an unforgettable photograph. As one looks carefully at the picture, four figures united by a rope are spotted in the shadows. Two are standing on the floor of the canyon while the other two are perched on the roof of the cliff house.

Timothy O'Sullivan was a true craftsman. His work was marked by the very great care he took in setting up his pictures and by the way in which he used light to achieve the effects he desired. When one considers the vast territory that O'Sullivan covered, the nature of the terrain over which he journeyed, and the physical hardships he endured to capture his inspiring views, it is apparent that his place is secure for all time as one of the most remarkable of the world's photographers.

While Carlton E. Watkins was the first of the great landscape photographers and Timothy O'Sullivan was undoubtedly the most spectacular, the Western photographer whose work became most influential in his own time was William Henry Jackson. This was because Jackson, unlike most of the other Western photographers, kept detailed diaries of his work and spent a good deal of time promoting himself and his photographs.

William H. Jackson, who had spent his early years in New England, went west in 1866 as an ox-team driver in a train of freight wagons. In 1867 he and his brother Edward went into the photography business in Omaha, Nebraska. They operated in a way similar to other commercial photographers throughout the United States, taking portraits, pictures of clubs and other groups, and of places of business. In 1864 Jackson decided to leave Omaha and follow the route of the Union Pacific Railroad. His plan was to earn his living by taking photographs all along the way and then selling them to the people who were pouring into the towns along the route of the railroad. He was earning a moderate income doing just this when he was introduced to Dr. F. V. Hayden, a

William H. Jackson
Canyon of the Mancos
1874

man who was about to lead another of the government's geological surveys into the unsettled territories.

For the next eight years Jackson was part of seven F. V. Hayden expeditions into the West. His travels took him across the eastern front of the Rocky Mountains, from New Mexico to Wyoming. He had little experience in landscape photography when the expedition began, but by the end of the first year he was capturing striking images on his eleven-by-fourteen-inch glass plates.

In 1873 the Hayden expedition was high in the mountains of Colorado, where Jackson took close-ups of Gray's Peak, Pike's Peak, and Torrey's Peak—the very summits of the Rocky Mountains. By this time he was an accomplished landscape photographer. He was also becoming more sensitive to the people who lived in the territory he was photographing. Toward the end of his years with the Hayden expedition, he took many pictures of the Indians who were still living in the areas where their ancestors had lived some three thousand years before.

In 1877 the Hayden expedition's field of operation was the region known as Yellowstone. Here Jackson took some of his most beautiful photographs. In photo after photo he caught the marvels of one of nature's most extraordinary areas. F. V. Hayden reproduced nine of Jackson's best pictures and bound them into gold-embossed volumes, which he then presented to each member of the United States Senate and House of Representatives. After viewing Jackson's photographs and staring in awe and amazement at the scenes they recorded, members of Congress introduced a bill

William H. Jackson
Ladore Canyon
c. 1870

80

designed to make Yellowstone the nation's first national park. The bill was ultimately passed, and thanks to Jackson's photographs and Hayden's initiative, one of America's most beautiful areas was saved from commercial exploitation for all time.

When his work with Hayden was completed, Jackson opened a studio in Denver. From there he sold his nature views to customers all over the world. He sold them on stereographic cards, and in large prints that could be framed. His photographs made people all over the world aware of the astonishing beauty of the American West.

There were, of course, other frontier photographers whose work was of the highest quality. The names of such men as Layton Huffman, Frank Jay Haynes, J. C. H. Grabil, and William Bell deserve an honored place in the ranks of America's best early photographers.

William H. Jackson and Timothy O'Sullivan had completed their expeditionary work by the late 1870s. By that time the combat pictures of Mathew Brady and the other Civil War photographers were already more than fifteen years old. Photography itself had been in existence for barely forty years. What extraordinary progress had been made in such a short period of time! The Civil War photographers and the skilled photographers of the West had seized upon the moment and had advanced a new form of art farther and more quickly than anyone could have imagined possible.

S. R. Stoddard
The Scientists
Dry-plate photograph
1889

Three

Photography for the Millions

THE PHOTOGRAPHS taken by the cameramen of the West are remarkable documents. The fact that the wet plates upon which they were taken had to be developed immediately, no matter where the photographers found themselves, makes their accomplishments even more remarkable. While the wet-plate process was a tremendous improvement over all that had come before it, the task of producing a good photograph was still a difficult one. It was a messy job, as well. Many early photographic manuals contained detailed instructions on how to remove from carpets and furniture the spots that were caused by the tacky chemicals that dripped off the wet plates.

The first of a series of important new discoveries that in a few short years would put cameras in the hands of millions of Americans from coast to coast took place in 1871, and the person responsible for it was an Englishman named Dr. Richard L. Maddox. In

1871 he announced the perfection of a new photographic plate that used *gelatin* instead of collodion. Once the gelatin dried, it produced a dry plate, rather than a wet plate. As with all new inventions, there were certain "bugs" in Maddox's process that needed to be worked out. By 1880 this had been done, and photographers everywhere turned to the new dry-plate process.

Dry plates had tremendous advantages over the now old-fashioned wet plates. The photographer was no longer a slave to his darkroom. Since the dry plates could be developed at any reasonable time after they were taken, portable darkrooms were no longer necessary. The exposure time for the new plate was much faster than with the old process, so cameras could now be held in the hand rather than on cumbersome tripods. Moreover, since the dry plates did not have to be developed right away, they could be brought to others for developing. Up to this point the photographer had had to make his own plate, take the photograph, and then develop it immediately. Now two of these important processes could be turned over to others. Soon companies devoted exclusively to manufacturing dry plates began to make their appearance. Companies set up to develop prints also burst upon the scene. The whole photo-finishing industry was born. Dry plates were more expensive than wet plates, but photographers everywhere recognized the advantages in using them. By 1880 almost all photographers, amateurs and professionals, were using the new process.

As Maddox was perfecting his dry plates, another important development in photography was taking place—the capture of

Charles H. Currier
Family Portrait
Dry-plate photograph
1895

motion. Because of the long exposure time required, action could not be recorded in the earliest photographs. The first pictures that showed a moving subject as more than a blur were some of the stereographic views taken of busy city streets. In the 1870s, however, a major breakthrough became a reality. The man responsible for this breakthrough was Eadweard Muybridge, who, as noted, had begun his career as a photographer of the West.

In 1872 Muybridge was hired by Leland Stanford, a wealthy former governor of California, to help Stanford win a bet. Stanford owned a string of racehorses, including a famous trotter named Occident. He had bet a friend twenty-five thousand dollars that while a horse was in full stride, it had all four feet off the ground. Since this couldn't be detected by the naked eye, it had been assumed that horses, even in full stride, always had at least one foot on the ground.

In order to prove Stanford's contention, Muybridge used a fast shutter that he had invented and covered the background of the running track with white sheets in order to give him extra light. Then, using a single camera he took a series of pictures of Occident racing down the track. The wet plates that Muybridge used required too long an exposure time to give definite proof that Stanford was right, but there was enough indication in these early photos to convince him to ask Muybridge to continue the work. Meanwhile, the photographer became involved in other pursuits and was not able to continue his experiments for five years.

In 1878 Muybridge was ready to try again. In June of that year Stanford invited a group of San Francisco reporters to be present as Muybridge photographed a racing mare named Sallie Gardner.

This time Muybridge set up twelve cameras for the event. Each had a shutter that was triggered by a spring or rubber band. Twelve thin black threads were stretched across the track so that they would strike the mare breast high, releasing the shutter of each camera as she passed by. The wet plates that Muybridge used this time had been specially prepared to reduce the exposure time.

The photographs that resulted were everything that Stanford and Muybridge had hoped for. They proved beyond a shadow of a doubt that there is a time when a racehorse in full gallop has all four feet bunched under its belly, completely off the ground. Muybridge's series of photographs accomplished much more than merely allowing Stanford to win his bet. Artists all over the world were influenced by his series of pictures entitled "The Horse in Motion." Frederic Remington and Charles Russell, two famous painters of life in the West, changed the whole way they painted horses after viewing Muybridge's photographs.

In March of 1880 the San Francisco Art Association, by means of a special magic lantern, used Muybridge's series of pictures to project images of a galloping horse upon a large screen. The audience was amazed. What they were actually seeing was the first motion picture. Muybridge was dedicated to perfecting the technique of capturing movement in still photographs. By this time he had the use of the gelatin dry plate at his command. He spent most of the rest of his photographic career taking thousands of pictures of human beings and animals in motion, continually experimenting with new ways to freeze movement in the camera's eye.

Muybridge's achievements caught the attention of artists and

The Horse in Motion

Eadweard Muybridge
The Horse in Motion
1878

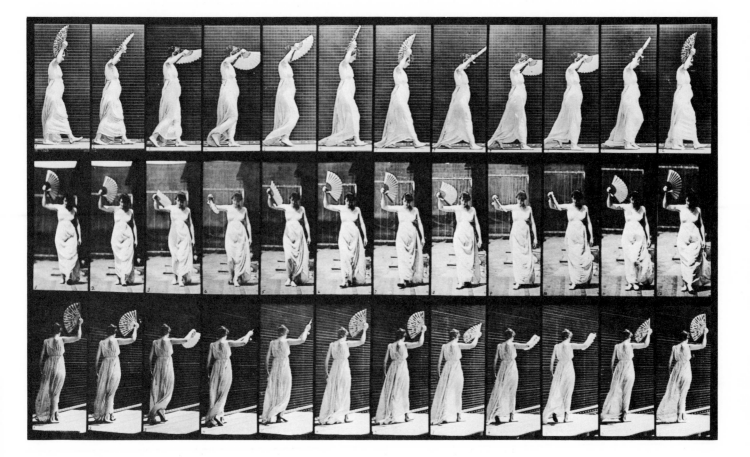

Eadweard Muybridge
Animal Locomotion
1887

photographers everywhere. Perhaps the most notable of these was the renowned American painter Thomas Eakins. A dedicated photographer as well as a painter, Eakins began to correspond with Muybridge. He arranged for them to work together in Pennsylvania, but they soon had a disagreement over what was the best method of capturing a moving subject photographically. Eakins was a trained scientist who had spent much time studying human and animal anatomy. He became convinced that, while Muybridge's use of a series of cameras to capture motion had been an important achievement, it failed to depict the subject exactly. Eakins felt that this had to be done by using a single camera. Eakins designed such a camera. He put a revolving disk in front of his lens. This disk had a hole in it that allowed several images to be taken on one glass plate. Eakins's theory was that a sequence of actions could be captured more naturally this way than by photographing separate actions with several cameras.

Like Muybridge, Eakins devoted much time to photographing people in motion—walking, pole-vaulting, carrying objects. Even though these motion studies and his painting kept him very busy, Eakins found the time to take other photographs of all types. His photographs are marked by the same attributes he brought to his painting. He was able to capture his subjects in such a way as to reveal their innermost nature. His portraits were so revealing, in fact, that one of Eakins's friends once stated that he would never allow Eakins to photograph him because "he would bring out all those traits of character that I have been trying to conceal for years."

Thomas Eakins
Pole-Vaulter
1884

The experiments of Muybridge and Eakins played an important role in the history of photography. Not only were they the first to analyze movement with a camera, but their experiments contributed to the development of faster shutters, smaller cameras, shorter exposure times, and other significant technical advances.

By the 1880s these technical improvements included a wide range of hand-held cameras. These box-shaped cameras, used mostly by amateurs to make candid shots, were often called "detective cameras." They got this name because in the late 1880s it was not considered proper etiquette to approach a stranger and ask permission to take a photograph. And it was deemed totally improper to take a picture without a subject's permission. Thus there was a demand for a camera that could be used without being detected. This demand was met by the creation of a variety of cameras that could be easily hidden. Tiny cameras were concealed in hats, canes, binoculars, and stickpins. The shutter was worked by a string or bulb housed in the operator's pocket.

This emphasis on the hand-held camera led to the invention of the most popular and famous camera ever produced—George Eastman's Kodak. Eastman was one of the earliest makers of dry plates in America. His dry-plate factory in Rochester, New York, continued to grow until it was a hugely successful business. Eastman was a creative genius who never stopped experimenting. Even though he was selling dry plates by the thousands, he began searching for a new type of negative that would be less cumbersome and expensive than glass plates. After a long series of experiments, Eastman perfected a roll of paper, which was coated

Thomas Eakins
Two Girls in Greek Dress
c. 1880

with two layers of gelatin. This "American film," as it was called, was completely flexible. A roll holder for the film could be adapted to any existing camera.

George Eastman's photographic experiments continued, and in 1888 he announced an invention that, combined with the flexible film he had perfected earlier, formed the basis for all of the material and equipment that are used in photography today. This invention was the Kodak. The Kodak was a small box camera. It was slightly over six inches long, three and a half inches wide, and less than four inches high. It was the most easily operated camera that had ever been developed. The instructions, according to the Kodak manual, were: 1. Point the camera. 2. Press the button. 3. Turn the key. 4. Pull the cord.

The Kodak was a completely sealed camera. It contained a roll of one hundred negatives that produced circular pictures two and a quarter inches in diameter. When all the negatives had been exposed, the owner sent the camera to the Eastman factory. There the camera was opened, mounted prints were made from the negatives, and a new roll of film was inserted. All of this was shipped back to the customer at a cost of ten dollars. The original purchase price of the Kodak itself was twenty-five dollars.

George Eastman's slogan for his Kodak was, "You press the button, we do the rest." All over the world people followed these instructions. Eastman had done for the camera what Henry Ford was later to do for the automobile. He had made it available to people everywhere. Professional photographers would continue to capture images on the larger, dry glass plates, but amateurs

Fred Church
George Eastman with Kodak Camera
1890

around the globe would soon be taking candid shots of family, friends, and activities with their ever-present Kodaks. Photography had become a folk art for the millions.

Unknown photographers
Early Kodak photographs
1889

Ulrich Bourgeois
Girl with Kodak
c. 1900

John J. Wright
The Photographers
c. 1895

John J. Wright
The Photographers
c. 1895

Four

Photography As Art

THE CAMERAMEN whose work we have examined thus far were, for the most part, totally consumed with capturing likenesses of people great and small and with recording scenes and events all over America. Few of them would have taken the time to become deeply involved in such a question as whether or not photography was really art. Yet by the 1890s such a question was being seriously raised in both Europe and America.

The many advancements made in cameras, negatives, and printing methods gave photographers more options than ever before in the way they took and printed their pictures. In England, for example, some people began to produce photographs that were to them more important for the technique they employed than for their subject matter. These cameramen and -women, often called *pictorialists*, used soft focusing, intense whites, and dark shadows in their work and developed their prints on highly textured papers. A new process called *gum-bichromate* was also used, which allowed

Alvin Langdon Coburn
Harbor Scene
c. 1915

100

the photographer to work much like a painter. He or she could apply silver salts to the negative with a brush or wash away part of the negative to achieve desired results. Many of these "art photographs" actually resembled charcoal drawings or watercolors. A journal of the day stated, "[There] is no limit to what a photographer can do to make a photograph a work of art. . . . Meddling with a gum print may or may not add the vital spark, though without the meddling there will surely be no spark whatever."

This question of "meddling" with photographs was to become a serious issue. In America brilliant young photographers such as Alvin Langdon Coburn and Clarence White produced pictures that looked more like paintings than photographs. And in 1902 Alfred Stieglitz, perhaps the most brilliant America photographer of all time, stated that it was "justifiable to use any means upon a negative of paper to attain the desired end."

Stieglitz was soon to change his opinion, and eventually all of the negatives he took were untouched. The prints he made from them were uncropped and as true to the negatives as possible. Stieglitz became the most influential of all American photographers, for while he cherished the beautiful qualities of paintings, he recognized that photography could be true art only if its strength lay in photographs that had great artistic validity without being imitations of paintings. This was what distinguished his work from that of the pictorialists. Soon the term "straight photography" was applied to that type of photographic style upon which Stieglitz was to have such an important influence.

Clarence White
The Ring Toss
c. 1903

Alfred Stieglitz once declared, "I was born in Hoboken, New Jersey. I am an American. Photography is my passion. The search for truth is my obsession." As a young man, Stieglitz went to Germany to study mechanical engineering. While passing a Berlin shop window, he saw a camera, which he bought. Soon he found himself much more interested in photography than in engineering. He took many pictures, and early in his career the prestigious Viennese gallery known as the Vienna Salon exhibited several of his photographs.

Upon returning to America, Stieglitz found that photography was flourishing. There were camera clubs everywhere, and countless amateurs were taking pictures of every possible subject. But to Stieglitz's dismay, there was no organized group dedicated to working to make photography recognized as a legitimate art form.

Toward this end, in 1886 he joined the Camera Club of New York and transformed the club's journal into a publication called *Camera Notes*. It contained marvelous reproductions of photographs by both members and nonmembers, and eventually became the most important and influential photographic journal of its kind. Stieglitz meanwhile had become annoyed with the conservative practices of the Camera Club. He resigned, and along with others formed a group of his own known as the Photo-Secession. The official publication of this group was *Camera Work*, and Stieglitz was its editor and publisher. The Photo-Secession group stated that its goals were "to hold together those Americans devoted to pictorial photography, . . . to exhibit the best that has been accomplished by its members or other photographers, and, above all, to dignify that profession until recently looked upon as a trade."

In 1905 the Photo-Secession opened a gallery at 291 Fifth Avenue in New York. For the next twelve years the gallery gave photographers the opportunity to display their work alongside that of some of the finest painters and sculptors in the world, and 291 (or the Little Galleries) became one of the most influential art galleries in America. Through it, Stieglitz found an outlet for one of his strongest desires—to have photography accepted as a true art form.

Meanwhile, Stieglitz himself took some of the most striking and important photographs the world had ever known. One, entitled "The Steerage," is regarded by some art historians as perhaps the finest single photograph ever taken. On a voyage to Europe in 1907, Stieglitz, who was traveling first class, happened to look down upon the steerage, that section where passengers paying the lowest fare were herded together like cattle. Stieglitz's own description of how he came to take the picture reveals his intensity as an artist and is a classic statement about how a master photographer views his subject and how a great photograph is born.

Coming to the end of the deck [he later recalled], I looked down. There were men, women and children on the lower level of the steerage. A narrow stairway led up to a small deck at the extreme bow of the steamer. A young man in a straw hat, the shape of which was round, gazed over the rail, watching a group beneath him. To the left was an inclining funnel. A gangway bridge, glistening with fresh white paint, led to the upper deck.

The scene fascinated me. A round straw hat, the funnel leaning left, the stairway leaning right; the white drawbridge, its railings made of chain: white suspenders crossed on the back of a man below; circular iron machinery; a mast that cut into the sky, completing the triangle. I stood spellbound. I saw shapes relating to one another—a picture of shapes, and underlying it, a new vision that held me: simple people; the feeling of ship, ocean, sky: a sense of release that I was away from the mob called rich. . . .

I raced to the main stairway of the steamer, chased down to my cabin, picked up my Graflex, raced back again, worrying whether or not the man with the straw hat had shifted his position. If he had, the picture I saw would no longer exist.

The man with the straw hat had not stirred an inch. Neither had the man with the crossed suspenders. The woman with the child on her lap remained on the floor motionless.

I had only one plate holder with one unexposed plate. Could I catch what I saw and felt? I released the shutter. If I had captured what I wanted, the photograph would go far beyond any of my previous prints. It would be a picture based on related shapes and deepest human feeling. . . .

When we reached Paris I tried at once to find out where I might develop my plate. I was given the address of a photographer who led me to a huge darkroom. . . . I developed, washed, and rinsed the plate. Held up to the red light it seemed all right, yet I would not be sure until it had been completely fixed. At last I could turn on the white light. The negative was perfect in every particular. . . .

Some months later, after *The Steerage* was printed, I felt satisfied, something I have not been very often. When it was published, I felt that if all my photographs were lost and I were represented only by *The Steerage*, that would be quite all right.

Alfred Stieglitz
The Steerage
1907

Stieglitz always had a very strong feeling about nature. Many of his finest photographs were taken during warm-weather showers or winter snowstorms. A photograph such as "The Terminal" is brilliant for the way in which it draws the viewer into the scene and captures the mood of the image presented. In viewing this photograph, one almost seems to actually feel the snow and the cold.

The ability to express feelings was Stieglitz's strongest asset as a photographer. Of his experience in taking "The Terminal" he wrote, "There was snow on the ground. A driver in a rubber coat was watering his steaming horses. There seemed to be something closely related to my deepest feeling on what I saw, and I decided to photograph what was within me. The steaming horses and their driver watering them on a cold winter day; my feeling of aloneness in my own country, amongst my own people.... I felt how fortunate the horses were to have at least a human being to give them the water they needed. What made me see the watering of the horses as I did was my own loneliness."

This ability to transmit his own feelings through the photographs he took marked Stieglitz and his work all through his life. He used the term "equivalents" to express the relationship between what he felt and the images he captured. "When I see something that serves as an equivalent for what I am experiencing myself," he said, "then I feel compelled to set down a picture of it as an honest statement—which statement may be said to represent my feelings about life."

By 1925 Alfred Stieglitz had earned an international reputa-

Alfred Stieglitz
The Terminal
1893

Alfred Stieglitz
Paula
1889

110

Alfred Stieglitz
The Flatiron
1903

Alfred Stieglitz
Wet Day on the Boulevard, Paris
1894

tion. In that year the Anderson Galleries in New York held a showing of some of his works. Said one reviewer, "[These photographs] made me want to forget all the photographs I had seen before, and I have been impatient in the face of all the photographs I have seen since, so satisfying [were they] in those subtle qualities which constitute all we commonly call 'works of art.'"

Through his gallery, its publications, and his own camera work, Alfred Stieglitz influenced a whole group of American photographers whose work eventually brought them deserved recognition in their own right. For example, the last two issues of *Camera Work* carried photographs by a new photographer named Paul Strand. They included a powerful series in which form and design were stressed—a collection of bowls; a scene dominated by the vertical shapes in a white picket fence.

Strand's sense of poetry in the environment around him gave his photographs a special touch, a special meaning. He concentrated on photographing simple things, and the pictures he took of people displayed a sensitivity uniquely his own. One of his most famous photographs is that of a blind woman. As one studies the picture, one can understand what Strand meant when he said, "It is one thing to photograph people: it is another thing to make others care about them by revealing the core of their humanness."

A genuine craftsman, Strand used platinum paper in developing his prints. Even though this developing paper was costly and increasingly scarce, he used it as long as it was on the market because with it he was able to obtain maximum tone and bring out as much detail as possible from the negatives he exposed. Both

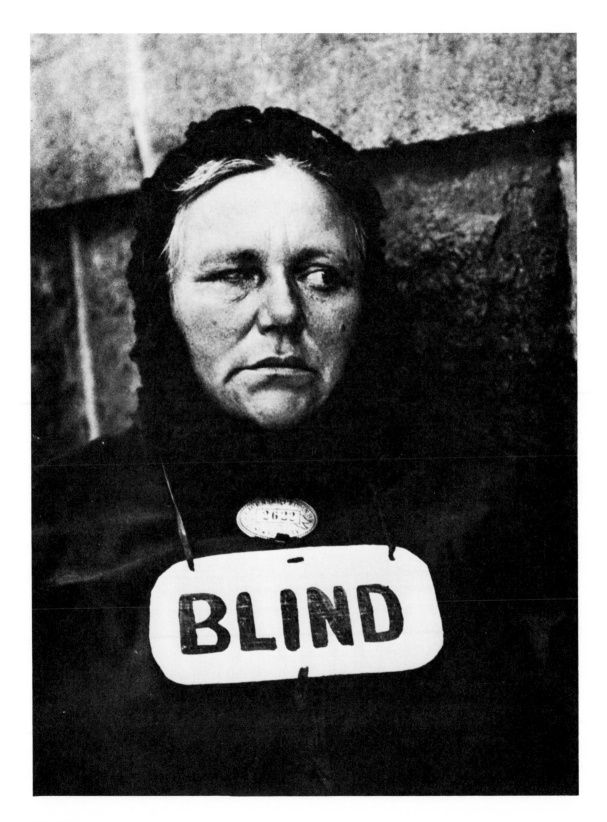

Paul Strand
Blind Woman
1916

behind the camera and in the darkroom he was a perfectionist—seeking simplicity and truth in all he did.

The man destined to become the most famous of all the young photographers influenced by Stieglitz was Edward Steichen. An original member of the Photo-Secession, Steichen became deeply involved in several branches of photography—and he proved to be a master of all of them. During World War I he was an aerial military photographer. After the war he became one of America's most successful fashion photographers. He made an important historical contribution in World War II by leading a United States Navy photographic department, which captured a remarkable pictorial record of the war at sea. After World War II he became director of photography for the Museum of Modern Art in New York. While there he organized "The Family of Man," the most popular photographic exhibition ever held. For this exhibition Steichen selected photographs from more than two million prints sent from photographers around the world.

As a photographer, Steichen, like other members of the Photo-Secession, started out as a pictorialist. As an aerial photographer in World War I, however, he had to produce pictures that were as clear and detailed as possible. This experience converted him to "straight" photography. When he returned home from the war, he devoted the better part of a year to taking thousands of pictures that would perfect his straight-photography technique.

Steichen had been trained as a painter, and this training plus his unique photographic skills enabled him to capture the very essence of those who sat for portraits before his camera. For example, his 1903 photograph of J. Pierpont Morgan is one of the most striking portraits ever taken (page 118). In all of his work, Steichen used light in such a way as to accentuate those features he wished to bring out in his subject. In this photograph the use of a dark background accentuates the stern face of the powerful financier. Morgan's gold watch and chain, symbols of wealth and position, are also accentuated by the dark background and his dark suit. And most important of all, a highlight on the arm of the chair in which Morgan sits looks for all the world like a dagger poised in the hand of the man who controlled the fate of so many people.

Steichen was a brother-in-law of the great American poet and writer Carl Sandburg. In another memorable photograph he created a dramatic study of his famous brother-in-law, capturing in one montage a variety of moods and expressions (page 119). Once again, his use of lighting dramatizes the unique features of his subject.

His use of lighting and his ability to contrast shades of white, gray, and black marked all of Steichen's photographs. Whether they were portraits, still lifes, fashion or action shots, they all carried this Steichen trademark. Steichen was a prolific photographer. He took thousands of commercial photographs for the nation's magazines. America's leading celebrities sat before his camera. He lived to the age of ninety-four, and continued his curatorial and photographic work almost until the day he died. It is no wonder that many people regard him as the "Dean of American Photography."

118

Edward Steichen
Carl Sandburg
1936

Edward Steichen
J. P. Morgan
1903

At the turn of the century those photographers working on the West Coast of America tended to photograph different types of subjects than did their counterparts in the East. While East Coast cameramen and -women concentrated heavily on city scenes, those in the still relatively undeveloped West often chose nature as their subject. This was true of Edward Weston, a Californian who became one of America's most highly regarded photographers.

Like others, Weston, early in his career, used many of the methods of the pictorialists. Some of his early photographs look a great deal like paintings. After becoming acquainted with Stieglitz, Strand, and other members of the Photo-Secession, however, he changed his style dramatically and he too became a practitioner of straight photography. Weston used an eight-by-ten-inch camera (that is, it produced images on eight-by-ten-inch plates) to capture his dramatic landscapes. The images he produced are notable for their great clarity and detail. They are marked also by the imagination he used in selecting his forms and subjects.

For Edward Weston almost everything in nature was a valid subject for his camera. Tangled tree stumps, shells, rocks—even vegetables. He was able to see sculpture in every form. To Weston the natural structure of a halved cabbage was as beautiful, dramatic, and photographically noteworthy as the most majestic mountains he also photographed. "The camera should be for a recording of life," he wrote, "...whether it be polished steel or palpitating flesh." It was his desire to capture the very essence of his subject, whatever he trained his camera upon. The subject, he said, "must be rendered with the utmost exactness: stone is

Edward Weston
Church Door, Hornitos
1940

Edward Weston
Sand Dunes
1936

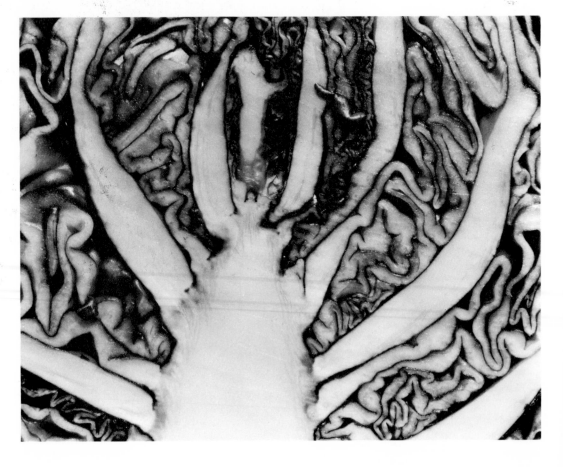

Edward Weston
Half Cabbage
1930

122

hard, bark is rough, flesh is alive." As one studies Weston's photographs, it becomes obvious that he remained true to this creed. And because he possessed talents that were uniquely his own, he was able to add a quality that went beyond this exactness. This quality lay in his ability to convey to the viewer the feeling that he really cared about the subject he was capturing.

Throughout his lifetime Weston had a profound influence on the field of photography. In 1932 he and some fellow photographers formed a society called Group f.64. They chose this name because "f.64" is a technical term used to denote a small lens opening. Members of Group f.64 used small lens openings in their cameras to achieve detailed images in their work. The original members of the society included such outstanding photographers as Imogen Cunningham and Ansel Adams. Group f.64 held many exhibitions and was, for years, the most progressive society of its kind in the country. In 1937 Weston was awarded a coveted John Simon Guggenheim Memorial Foundation Fellowship—the first ever to be given to a photographer. Like Stieglitz and Steichen, Edward Weston did much toward making American photography a recognized and accepted form of art.

Five

Early Documentary
Photography

IN THE LATTER YEARS of the nineteenth century most of the photographic journals focused their attention on the works of those photographers who have been labeled pictorialists. There were at that time, however, scores of photographers who were using their cameras in a much different way from the pictorialists. These men and women were making a conscious record of life and conditions in places all over America. Today we use the term *documentary* to describe the photographic record they produced, and we recognize their work as among the most important in all of photographic history.

From the time the first exposure was made, it was obvious that photographs could reveal and persuade in ways that had never been possible before. All of these documentary photographers sought to reveal particular life and work styles through their photographs. Some went one step farther. They sought through their pictures to convince and persuade private citizens and public agencies to take certain actions based on the evidence they presented in their photographs.

As previously noted, pioneer photographers of the American West introduced to the general public whole new areas of the nation that had never been revealed before. William H. Jackson's striking photographs convinced the United States Congress to set apart the Yellowstone region as a national park. As the nineteenth century came to an end, other photographers devoted themselves to other causes—often with equally rewarding results.

Foremost among these early documentary photographers was a Danish immigrant named Jacob A. Riis. A reporter for the New York *Evening Sun,* Riis was America's first journalist-photographer. He was well acquainted with and shocked by the teeming slums of New York City, and he accompanied his photographs of this squalor with dramatic written descriptions of the tenements, streets, and alleys where as many as 275,000 people per square mile lived under the most horrible conditions possible.

One of the worst sections of the city was an area known as Mulberry Bend. Riis called it "the foul core of New York's slums." He took many photographs of this section. They are marked by the suspicious faces of the adults, the pathetic conditions of the children, and the ever-present litter in the street below and the hanging laundry above.

Robbers' Roost in Mulberry Bend was one area that became a target for Riis's camera. The immigrants who lived there were involved in every type of crime. Riis photographed them standing

Jacob Riis
Baxter Street Court
c. 1895

Jacob Riis
Under the Porch
c. 1895

in their alleys, perched on windowsills, and huddled underneath tenement porches amid debris. On more than one occasion Riis literally had to flee for his life from subjects who did not want to become part of his documentaries. In books such as *How the Other Half Lives* and *Battle with the Slums*, Riis described the dangers he continually faced. For example: "Yet even from Hell's Kitchen had I not long before been driven forth with my camera by a band of angry women who pelted me with brickbats and stones on my retreat, shouting at me never to come back. . . ."

The abuses he took did not discourage Riis from his goal of revealing conditions that cried out for change. It was inside the tenements themselves where he found the worst squalor of all. He was one of the first photographers to use the magnesium flash in taking indoor pictures, and this new method played an important role in helping him gather his evidence of the horrors of tenement life. Describing the scene he encountered when taking a now-famous photograph entitled "Lodgers in a Bayard Street Tenement," he wrote, "In a room not thirteen feet either way slept twelve men and women, two or three in bunks set up in a sort of alcove, the rest on the floor. A kerosene lamp burned dimly in the fearful atmosphere probably to guide other and later arrivals to their beds, for it was just past midnight."

Like other great documentary photographers who followed him, Riis was careful to avoid degrading his subjects. Many of his pictures chronicle the noble attempt of individuals struggling against all odds to achieve some kind of civilized life amid the squalor around them. In one of his photographs, for example, he

Jacob Riis
"Five Cents a Spot"—Lodgers in a Bayard Street Tenement
c. 1900

captured the determination of a Jewish cobbler to carry on his traditional Sabbath dinner inside the coal cellar in which he lived. One of Riis's major photographic strengths was his ability to capture detail, and in this picture he not only shows the Sabbath bread laid out on the cleanest tablecloth the man could provide but also is careful to include at the left of the picture the homemade Yiddish sign with which the cobbler advertised his services.

Jacob Riis
*Ready for the
Sabbath Eve*
c. 1890

Of the thousands of photographs that Riis took, the most haunting and heartrending of all were those of the children of the slums. In their faces could be seen all the ills and evils that Riis so desperately sought to correct. It was the children who suffered most. In one year alone more than one hundred fifty youngsters under five years of age died in one city block. In a dramatic photography entitled "Street Arabs" Riis presented the nation with a

Jacob Riis
Street Arabs
c. 1900

picture of these youngsters seeking relief from their ice-cold tenement by sleeping next to a sidewalk grate. It is an example of the documentary camera at its best. It records for all to see a situation that stirs the emotions and cries out for reform.

Thanks in great part to Riis, reform did come. His photographic documents were published in nine books. They aroused the public to such a point that many tenements were torn down, schools were established for truants, and many squalid areas were cleaned up. As one historian has said, his photographs "contain qualities which will last as long as man is concerned with his brother."

The dedication and drive that marked the career of Jacob Riis were qualities that could be found in another important early documentary photographer. His name was Lewis Hine, and he used his camera to record, and to bring about reform in, a very specific area—child labor abuse. Hine was a trained sociologist who did not start taking photographs until he was thirty-seven years old. While still an amateur, he photographed immigrants at Ellis Island in New York, blacks in Washington, D.C., and coal miners in Pittsburgh. From the very beginning it was obvious that Hine was a true artist with the camera. One of his earliest photographs was that of a newly arrived Italian immigrant family looking for their luggage at Ellis Island. All immigrants had to pass through this island on their way into the United States. In the eyes and expressions of the mother and her children in the picture, Hine captured the anxieties and fears that accompanied all the newcomers as they were about to begin life in an unknown land

Lewis Hine
Immigrants Seeking Lost Baggage
1905

with unknown people. The way the photograph is balanced is another example of Hine's artistry. Whatever the subject, he had the ability to bring a unifying composition to all of his pictures. Thus, in this photograph the small child in his mother's arms on the left and the sack on the boy's shoulder at the right form a natural frame for the family group within.

Lewis Hine's main concerns as a sociologist and human being were the nearly two million children aged six to fourteen who were working ten hours a day or more in the nation's factories, mines, canneries, streets, and farms. He was determined to use his newfound photographic career to document this abuse of so large a portion of the nation's children. In 1908 he received his opportunity. The National Child Labor Committee hired him to make a photographic record of child labor to be shown to the United States Congress.

Hine responded with a series of photographs that shocked the country. He took his four-by-five camera inside the mills, the factories, the canneries, and the mines. He took picture after picture of child laborers at a time when almost 20 percent of the nation's children were employed at full-time jobs that were both dangerous and unhealthy. He went into the mines of Pennsylvania, where more than fourteen thousand children, most of whom were under eleven years of age, were employed. He took many photographs of conditions there. Among the most dramatic was his picture of "breaker boys" at work. These boys, all of whom were between the ages of eight and fourteen, sat on crude benches for ten or twelve hours every day as lumps of coal passed down a chute

Lewis Hine
Breaker Boys
c. 1910

at their feet. Their job was to pick out the pieces of slate that had been mixed in with the coal. One mine foreman declared, "There are twenty boys in that breaker and I bet you could shake fifty pounds of dust out of their systems."

The majority of child workers in America labored in the nation's mills and factories. There they worked from sunup to sundown for pennies a day. For most of them, education was out of the question. They would spend their whole lives at work in the mill. Hine's powerful photographs of these youngsters were enhanced by the way he composed his pictures. He often used the contrast between the size of the child and the size of the machine to dramatize the situation. And, like all good photographers, he added a sense of mystery to his pictures whenever he could. Thus, he captures an unforgettable image of a child textile worker as she pauses for a moment to gaze out the factory window. What does she see? What is she thinking about?

The children that Hine photographed were employed at almost every conceivable task. They worked in quarries, on fishing vessels, in lumber camps—everywhere. The streets of the nation's cities were filled with youngsters at work. They shined shoes, sold vegetables, and hauled goods from factory to store. In the South thousands of young children were employed by the oyster and shrimp canneries. This was a particularly difficult job. Oyster shuckers, for example, stood all day long in the same spot on a cold, wet floor. The oyster shells could cause horrible cuts on fingers and hands. For enduring all this the children were paid five cents for filling up a pail with oysters. The most they could hope to fill in a day was two pails.

As we look at Hine's photographs of these children, our attention is drawn to his fine sense of contrast and detail. He photographs a child pushing a loaded handcart down the street. Is it an accident that he photographs the child laborer in front of a store where diamonds are being sold? And as we look closely at his photograph of oyster shuckers at work, we suddenly notice the terribly young worker at the extreme left of the picture. Hine has reminded us that we must look carefully at every photograph to get its full impact.

Hine was interested in more than just the negative aspects of American life. Along with his child-labor pictures, he took hundreds of photographs of adults proudly at their work, including a striking series of photographs of the men who built the Empire State Building. But it is the child-labor pictures for which he will be best remembered. Thanks largely to his efforts, protective child-labor laws were eventually passed. Like Jacob Riis, he had turned his camera into a powerful humanitarian weapon. Probably no one ever expressed the purposes of the documentary photographer better than Hine did when he said of his work, "There were two things I wanted to do. I wanted to show the things that had to be corrected. I wanted to show the things that had to be appreciated."

Joseph Byron was a talented photographer who had emigrated to the United States from England. He had five children, one of whom, a son named Percy, was to become his photographic partner. Percy was only eleven years old when his father began to

Lewis Hine
Boy with Handcart
c. 1910

Lewis Hine
Oyster Shuckers
c. 1910

Lewis Hine
Mill Hands
c. 1910

teach him the art of photography. By the time he was fourteen he had sold a picture to one of the nation's major newspapers. The photographs taken by the Byrons were in direct contrast to those taken by Riis and Hine. The Byrons photographed the rich, people who were anxious to have their pictures taken. The world was theirs and they knew it and they wanted it recorded for all time.

Of all the photographs the Byrons took of the wealthy at their leisure, perhaps the most striking is the scene of the well-dressed, well-fed gentlemen at a New York dinner party in 1900 (page 142). There they are—business tycoons, railroad magnates, shipping czars—the beneficiaries of the industrial revolution that made the United States the most prosperous nation on earth. The Byrons have captured them with all the trappings of their power. Tuxedos, cigars, plush surroundings—they are all there. In this as in many other photographs, the Byrons have caught the true spirit of the successful nineteenth-century businessman and hero, right down to the laurel wreath upon his head.

Along with capturing the rich at play, the Byrons left another photographic legacy—one that has been an important contribution of many documentary photographers. These were the scores of pictures they took of the homes of the wealthy; for the rapidly vanishing architecture of this country includes not only the homes of the early frontier settlers or the ornate public buildings that once were an important part of the national landscape but also the incredible mansions in which, in an age of huge fortunes and no income taxes, the wealthy housed themselves.

The Byrons' photograph of the Cornelius Vanderbilt mansion

Joseph Byron
Harrison Grey Fiske Dinner
1900

142

Joseph Byron
Cornelius Vanderbilt House
c. 1900

in New York City (page 143) is an important document of an age that has vanished. This incredible building, covering half a city block, required a staff of thirty servants to keep it in order. When the Byrons went there to take a series of photographs of the home, they discovered a remarkable fact of Vanderbilt life. All of the work done in the house had to be completed by the staff by nine in the morning. In this way, no Vanderbilt would be offended by having to look upon a member of the servant class.

Unlike Jacob Riis and Lewis Hine, the Byrons were not driven by a cause. They took their photographs for profit plain and simple. Still, some of the images they captured were real works of art, and they left a documentary record of an important aspect of turn-of-the-century American life. Their photograph of the cabstand at Madison Square in New York is a prime example. This picture is attributed to Joseph but may well have been taken by Percy. In any event, it is a beautiful image demonstrating the photographer's sense of composition and use of light. The shadows on the walk and road balance the delicate lines of the branches and leaves above. The slight motion in the ladies' garments at the left serves as a counterpoint to the stillness of the horses and driver at the right.

At the time the photographers represented in this section were taking their pictures, no one would have thought to have called them documentary photographers. Like so many periods, events, or people in history, they were not labeled until years afterward. Yet they all had one thing in common. They were determined to record a particular way of life for all to see. Such a person was

Joseph Byron
Stand at Madison Square
c. 1900

Adam Vroman. Born in Illinois, Vroman was a successful bookstore owner, who prided himself on his collections of rare books and Japanese jade and ivory figures. His awareness of the necessity of recording the past led him into a whole new adventure— that of compiling a visual record of the Hopi and Zuñi Indians of the American Southwest before their ancient ways of life were gone forever.

The Indians Vroman photographed were not fierce warriors or brave and dashing horsemen. They were farmers and villagers whose ancestors had lived in America for thousands of years. They were extremely suspicious of all photographers, whom they called "shadow catchers." They believed that whoever captured a person's photographic image had control of that person's spirit. By living with them and adapting to their ways and by letting them use his camera to photograph him before he photographed them, Vroman slowly but surely won their friendship and confidence.

They were a simple and direct people and Vroman was perfectly suited to photograph them, for his was a simple and direct style of photography. As we look at a Vroman portrait of Zuñi water carriers, we might consider the words of one of America's most important photographers, Ansel Adams, who has said of Vroman's work: "There are no obvious efforts to create subjective effects— but much magic is there, inherent in both subject and image because of the honest selectivity of the photographer's eye and mind."

The Southwest Indians were a deeply religious people with com-

Adam Vroman
Zuñi Water Carriers
c. 1900

plex beliefs and customs. Unlike many other Indian tribes, however, they were permanently settled into one region. This made
them increasingly accessible to tourists, and slowly through the
years white men's ways joined ancient customs as part of their
daily life. Vroman's documentary eye was quick to pick this out.
His photograph of the young Hopi group is a perfect example of
how he was able to capture its development. In the picture the
young men wear white-men's suspenders and jeans. On the other
hand, the "squash blossom" hairdos worn by the girls date back
more than a thousand years. They were the badges of unmarried
women and required much time and care to construct.

Like the Byrons, Adam Vroman left an important architectural
record of the people he photographed, although the structures
were as different as could be from those of wealthy Eastern white
Americans. The Southwest Indians lived in multiroomed villages
known as pueblos, which were located at the top of large mesas high
above the Indian farmlands. In order to get to the pueblos, one
had to climb long, narrow, dangerous paths that ran up the face
of sheer cliffs. For Vroman the climb was made even more difficult
because of the bulky photographic equipment and fragile glass
plates he needed to carry with him. Yet he persevered. With much
patience and great sensitivity he left us a record of a people who
were among the first human beings in all of North America.

The most famous of all photographers of the American Indian,
however, was Edward S. Curtis. The story of Edward S. Curtis
and his work is truly amazing. Perhaps because of increased
awareness of the treatment received by the Indians at the hands

of early American settlers, interest in Curtis's work is now at an all-time high. Even without this factor, however, there is no question that Curtis ranks among the most important of all documentary photographers.

Like Vroman, Edward Curtis was obsessed with the idea of capturing the portraits and recording the customs and ceremonies of the North American Indians before their traditional ways of life disappeared forever. Unlike Vroman, however, he was not content to concentrate on one or two particular tribes. His goal was no less than to compile a photographic record of all the North American Indian tribes he could reach and to publish this record in a multivolume set of books.

The energy and dedication he brought to this lifetime task are almost beyond belief. He visited more than eighty tribes and took more than forty thousand photographs. In the beginning he thought his work would take about fifteen years. It took more than thirty! The diary he kept of his experiences reveals how extraordinarily dedicated he and his staff were and how hard they worked.

"Our party consisted of four men," he wrote. "Breakfast hour was 7:30; beginning active work at 8:00, a half-hour for lunch, an hour for supper, then working until 1:00 A.M. This was done every day of the month until spring. I did not take a day off work during that time, the only interruption being a single trip to the post office, six miles away. I permitted mail to come to our camp but once a week and no newspapers were allowed. Every thought and every movement had to be given to the work."

Edward S. Curtis
Bow River Blackfoot
1926

Before attempting to photograph a tribe, Curtis would spend months studying its history and customs. He would consult with scholars who had special knowledge. Only when he was sure that he knew as much as he could about the tribe and its history would he set out to do the fieldwork necessary to take his photographs.

This care and preparation did not go unnoticed by the Indians. In the past those who had come to photograph or write about them had usually done so without any sense of Indian culture and with an eye toward quick profit. As Curtis said in his diary, "The ordinary investigator going among them to secure information for a magazine article they do not favor. But they have grasped the idea that this is to be a permanent memorial of their race, and it appeals to their imagination. Word passes from tribe to tribe about it. A tribe that I have visited and studied lets another tribe know that after the present generation has passed away, men will know from this record what they were like, and what they did, and the second tribe doesn't want to be left out. Tribes that I won't reach for four or five years yet have sent me word asking me to come and see them. . . ."

From the beginning much of Curtis's energy had to be devoted to raising the money necessary for so large an undertaking. In the first years of his work finances were a continual problem. At times, a lack of funds threatened to halt the entire operation. Fortunately, his work caught the eye of President Theodore Roosevelt, who in 1906 recommended the project to multimillionaire J. Pierpont Morgan. After viewing a selection of Curtis's photographs, Morgan agreed to provide seventy-five thousand dollars so that

Edward S. Curtis
Assiniboin Mother and Child
1926

Edward S. Curtis
Assiniboin Placating the Spirit of a Slain Eagle
1926

Edward S. Curtis
Blackfoot Travois
1926

Edward S. Curtis
The Old Arapaho Warrior
c. 1920

the work could continue. After Morgan died in 1913 his son continued to finance the project.

Tribe by tribe, Curtis continued his painstaking, important work. There were hardships to be endured. Again from his diary: "At dark a terrific storm struck the camp. . . . Five Indian ponies in the neighborhood were killed by lightning. The equipment wagon got stuck in the mud in the middle of the White River and had to be taken apart before it [could be] got out. To the traveller such experiences are not so serious as to the photographer, for the results of many months of hard work may be lost in a moment by a careless driver."

There was criticism to endure as well. Despite his research and all the care he took in his work, Curtis became the target of some academics who were concerned with the fact that at times he had dressed some of the Indians in wigs and provided them with other long-vanished trappings of earlier days. Curtis readily admitted that while photographing the Indians of the Pacific Northwest he had done so. By the time he had reached these Indians, their ways of life had been drastically altered by white civilization. Their hair was now worn short and their once common practice of wearing abalone shells had been discarded. Curtis was determined to photograph them as they once were. Thus he had them put on wigs that were legitimate representations of their earlier hairstyles.

In spite of all the hardships and criticism, Curtis never lost sight of his goal. Cheyenne, Arapaho, Atsina, Yakima, Klickitat —he studied and photographed them all. And the photographs he produced were magnificent. Working with a huge fourteen-by-seventeen camera, he captured portraits and scenes on his glass negatives that will never be forgotten—chiefs on horseback, tribal members in front of teepees, Indians with ancient relics such as moose horns. His particular genius, however, was in taking portraits. He was able to use natural light in such a way as to capture the true spirit of every subject he took. As one critic has said, "Curtis worked as a cartographer, reading each face as a map of the past and of the character of each sitter. Unlike other Indian photographers who had photographed their subjects without attention to environment, Curtis sought always to bring out the individual qualities of the men, women and children before his lens."

After thirty years of work, with his health all but broken, Curtis completed his task. Twenty volumes of photographs and text and twenty portfolios of unbound prints were published under the title *The North American Indians*. A major New York newspaper called it "the most gigantic undertaking in the printing of books since the King James edition of the Bible." Curtis had achieved his dream. He had completed a photographic endeavor that remains unequaled in the annals of American photography.

Adam Vroman and Edward S. Curtis were determined to document the ways of the North American Indian before they passed forever from the American scene. In a like manner two other early documentary photographers devoted much of their lives to recording other ways of American life before they, too, disappeared. The first of these photographers was a man named Solomon Butcher.

He was a man with a vision. He had seen the Nebraska frontier area he loved slowly changing from open, endless prairie to the nation's most rapidly growing farm area. He became possessed with the idea of compiling a book of photographs and words that would capture the people, the sod houses, and the land of the American pioneers. "From the time I thought of the book," he said, "for seven days and seven nights it drove sleep from my eyes."

The prairie sod of the Nebraska frontier was the best farmland in the world. There were no rocks in it such as in the farmlands of the East and there were no trees such as those that farmers in other areas had to clear before they could begin farming. There were just miles and miles of open prairie. These Nebraska pioneers had two vital problems. One was loneliness. The other was how to construct their houses when no trees were available.

They found their answer in what they called a "soddy"—a house made of earth. The prairie turf was matted with thick grass roots. It held together like heavy rubber. The Nebraska settlers chopped the sod into bricklike strips and built their homes out of this material.

Two entities dominated the Nebraska landscape—endless prairie and sod houses. It was natural that they would dominate the photographs Butcher took as he made his way from homestead to homestead. In photograph after photograph we see these simple, rugged people posed with their children, their animals, their proudest possessions. Often there are distinguishing objects laid on the roofs of the sod houses. The prairie had so few landmarks that while in the fields a farmer could lose sight of his own house

Solomon Butcher
Family Group
1886

without an old chair or an animal's horns perched on the roof to guide him home.

Butcher was not interested in photography as art. His goal was to document his neighbors and their way of life. But he had a real sense of the dramatic, which is evident in the way he arranged his

subjects for his pictures. Men, women, children, horses, wagons, cattle, simple furniture—and the ever-present sod house—they are all arranged in such a way as to leave a permanent and unforgettable impression of a unique way of American life.

In one of his photographs Butcher's sense of the dramatic is almost eerie. His picture of the childless farm couple provides us with a study of two pioneers whose faces seem to reflect all of the hardships, determination, suffering, and pride that characterized the hardy people who made America. The pitchfork in the man's hand adds to the impact of the photograph. It takes on its eeriness when we realize how remarkably similar this photograph is to one of the most famous pictures ever painted in this country—Grant Wood's *American Gothic*. Butcher's photograph was taken some forty years before Wood even conceived his masterpiece.

While Solomon Butcher was preserving on glass a way of life that was slowly vanishing, another documentary photographer was doing the same thing in another part of the country. His name was Erwin Smith and his subject was the most famous of all the nation's folk heroes—the American cowboy. Smith, who was born in Texas, was fascinated with the life of the open range. He wanted to be a sculptor and was determined to train himself in this art so that he could carve images of the cowboys. When he was eighteen years old, he went to Chicago to study. After two years there, however, he realized that the range and the ways of life of the American cowboy were disappearing so fast that there soon would be nothing of the cowboy's way of life left to sculpture. He bought himself a Kodak, returned to Texas, and took

Solomon Butcher
Couple
1886

almost two thousand photographs of cowboys at work. His pictures provide us with the best firsthand views we have of a true American legend.

Perhaps the most important reason that Smith's photographs of the American cowboy are the best ever taken is that he actually worked alongside the cowboys on ranches and the open range. He had his camera strapped to his saddle and it went wherever he rode. Each evening before he went to bed, he would make a rough pencil sketch of the composition of photographs he hoped he would take the next day. He found it necessary to do this because his experience taught him that the nature of the cowboys' work rarely gave them time to stop to pose for photographs.

Smith had the ability, even with his relatively simple Kodak, to capture motion. One of his best-known pictures is that of a cowpoke straining to "pull in" a rearing horse. The action takes place in the foreground of the photograph, while a chuck wagon and then a large range of mountains form a backdrop for the picture.

Most of Smith's pictures are marked by motion, activity, and the ever-present dust kicked up by the moving herd. Many are simply beautiful photographs. The cowboy sits high in his saddle; the trail herd moves slowly along; sagebrush and mountains form natural backdrops and frames for the pictures.

More than anything else, Smith was determined to document the cowboy at work. By the time he began photographing the West, stories and books were already being written depicting cowboy life as one in which most of the day was spent in fighting In-

Erwin Smith
Lassooing Horse
c. 1905

Erwin Smith
Roundup
c. 1905

Erwin Smith
In Camp
c. 1905

Erwin Smith
At the Bar
c. 1905

dians, chasing outlaws, and saving heroines from bad men seeking to swindle them out of their land. Smith's photographs show the cowboys as they really were—men with important and often difficult work to do. He recorded every aspect of their life—rounding up the cattle, branding them, herding them, driving them to market. He showed them at campfires, at the chuckwagon, on the ranch, on the range, and in town. His was a complete record of another vanishing way of American life.

With all of his determination to show the cowboy at work, it is to Smith's credit that he was also able to record the very real aspect of the cowboy as a romantic figure. One of his most memorable photographs shows cowhands lined up at a bar in Old Tascosa, Texas. Leather chaps, spurs, tall hats, whiskey bottles on the bar—an authentic model for hundreds of movies and television series to come.

Early American documentary photographers came from every kind of background and every walk of life. One of the most interesting of them was a man named Arnold Genthe. Born to a wealthy family in Germany, Genthe came to America to tutor the son of a wealthy San Francisco couple. He was a highly educated man who had a wide range of interests, including painting and music.

Soon after he arrived in San Francisco, he became fascinated with the romance and mystery of the Chinatown section of that city. In the late 1800s this area was really an Oriental city within the confines of San Francisco itself. The first Chinese had come to California in great numbers in the 1850s, looking for gold. They found upon their arrival that they were legally banned from digging for the precious metal. Forced to find other means of support, some opened restaurants, others took in washing, or scratched out a living at whatever task they could find. Between 1864 and 1869 many went to work laying tracks for the transcontinental railroad.

At the time Genthe arrived, there were some twenty thousand people living in Chinatown. In 1882 the United States government had passed an act virtually banning any further Chinese immigration into the country. The people of Chinatown drew themselves in and built a life practically shut off from the outside world.

Genthe was determined to record this world. At first he tried to do this with his sketch pad. But whenever he would begin to draw, the people in the vicinity would quickly disappear into hallways and shops. The Chinese believed that anyone who drew a person's image could then work evil with it. Genthe was not to be deterred. He bought himself a small camera—"a black devil box," the Chinese called it—and by hiding in doorways and behind signs and columns, he managed to document the unique way of life in this area.

He photographed the people who lived and worked on streets with such names as "Street of the Butchers," "Street of the Sing-Song Girls," and "Street of the Gamblers." He would wander through the streets for hours and then take cover and pull his small camera from his pocket. Thus, the scenes he captured were really candid photographs. Genthe had such a brilliant eye for

Arnold Genthe
Street Scene
c. 1895

Arnold Genthe
The Butcher
c. 1895

composition, however, that the pictures that resulted seem almost too formal to possibly be candid shots.

As one studies, for example, the photograph he entitled "The Butcher," one is struck by its composition and balance. One is struck also by the expression on the meat cutter's face. Is it our imagination, or is he suspicious that someone might be taking his picture? Even in busy street scenes, Genthe was somehow able to achieve a balance and a unity not usually found in candid photographs.

Genthe's documentation of Chinatown life was made more important than anyone could have realized when on April 18, 1906, a tremendous earthquake struck San Francisco. Chinatown, along with much of the rest of the city, was wiped out. When the earthquake struck, Genthe's studio was immediately destroyed. He borrowed the first camera he could find—a simple 3A Kodak Special—and roamed the city, taking pictures of the collapsed buildings, the roaring fires, and the dazed people.

His earthquake photographs are incredible documents. Even in the midst of calamity, his candid shots reveal the same sense of balance and composition that the earlier Chinatown pictures contained. Perhaps it is true, as one art historian has said, that "a true artist is incapable of producing an unartistic piece of work."

Arnold Genthe had a long career in photography. He became a portrait photographer and some of the most famous people in America sat for him in his studio. But he will be best remembered for his two remarkable series of documentary photographs—those of Chinatown and the San Francisco earthquake.

Arnold Genthe
San Francisco Earthquake
1906

No study of early American documentary photography would be complete without including the work of an exceptional woman, Frances Benjamin Johnston. Born in 1864 to wealthy parents, Miss Johnston traveled easily between two worlds. A niece of Mrs. Grover Cleveland, she had access to the White House during the administrations of Presidents Cleveland, Benjamin Harrison, McKinley, Theodore Roosevelt, and Taft. Through these connections she was able to take photographs of some of the leading personalities of the day. But it was not the field of portraiture that interested her. Early in her career she saw the camera as a means of making important social statements.

In an era when few women were involved in such endeavors, she traveled to the coalfields of Pennsylvania and the factories of Lynn, Massachusetts, to record working conditions in those places. These pictures brought her such acclaim that she was asked to do a series of photographs of the Washington, D.C., public schools by officials of the prestigious Paris Exposition of 1900. At this time American public schooling was only sixty years old and there was great interest in how the educational system was working. The Paris commission gave her a backbreaking deadline, but she met it by producing seven hundred striking images in less than six weeks.

"The woman who makes photography profitable," she said, "must have good common sense, unlimited patience to carry her through endless failures, equally unlimited tact, good taste, a quick eye, and a talent for detail." This talent for detail was her special gift. Her photographs of the Washington schoolchildren are excellent examples of this gift. The photographs are obviously posed, yet they include such details and are composed in such a way as to make them unforgettable rather than trite. In a picture of students boarding a trolley car, for example, she framed different groups of students within the trolley's windows and doorway. As with so many of her pictures, many small photographs are contained within the photograph itself.

Her pictures were the hit of the Paris Exposition. She followed this success by joining Admiral George Dewey's fleet as it returned from its historic victory at Manila Bay, thus giving the nation its first views of life aboard the Great White Fleet.

But her greatest work was yet to come. In a time of bitter racism and little opportunity for black advancement, she accepted an invitation from Booker T. Washington, a former slave, and traveled to the South, where she recorded life at Hampton and Tuskegee institutes, two schools founded to train black students in skilled labor. There she photographed students learning to be cobblers, farmers, milliners, carpenters—tradesmen and -women of all kinds. She brought to these photographs the same sense of composition, the same sense of detail that had marked all of her previous work, and as one looks at these photographs, one can again find many striking pictures within pictures in each of them.

As we look at these Hampton and Tuskegee photographs today, it may seem to us that the aspirations of these students were very small. They were learning to be skilled laborers, not doctors or lawyers. In those days, however, the two schools represented the best hopes many blacks had for any advancement in segregated America.

That this was true can be seen in the photographs that Miss Johnston took immediately after completing her work at Hampton and Tuskegee. While in the South she traveled throughout the countryside, photographing black families living in conditions little improved from the days of slavery.

There was a special dignity in the images she presented of the rural black South. Her pictures helped make Americans aware of how much needed to be done before blacks could begin to gain equal rights and opportunities. Hers was the documentary camera at its very best, creating the awareness needed before reform could

Frances Benjamin Johnston
Children on Trolley
1899

Frances Benjamin Johnston
Millinery Class at Tuskeegee
1899

Frances Benjamin Johnston
Children
c. 1900

Frances Benjamin Johnston
Cobblers' Class at Tuskeegee
1902

begin. In many ways, Frances Benjamin Johnston symbolized all of the documentary photographers included in this section. Hard work, a sense of purpose, attention to detail, genuine photographic skill—they were all the tools of the true documentary photographers.

Frances Benjamin Johnston
Self-Portrait
1895

Six

Other Masters

STIEGLITZ, STEICHEN, RIIS—these and the other photographers whom we have considered thus far will be recognized forever as masters of their art. One of the most exciting and fascinating things about photography, however, is that it has been with us for such a relatively short time that whole bodies of photographers' work are still being discovered. Some of this work is of such high quality that it can stand equally alongside that of already recognized masters.

There is simply not enough space in any one history of photography to include descriptions of all the photographers whose work, although of the highest quality, has until recently received comparatively little attention. Some of these photographers were amateurs who had a special talent for photographing particular subjects. Others were professionals who in their lifetime never received the acclaim that we now know is due them. It is safe to say that at this very moment there are collections of the plates of other "unknown" masters lying in attics, basements, or old photographic studios waiting to be discovered.

In this section we will consider, as a sampling, selected works by seven individuals and one early photographic company—all of which are of such depth and quality that their creators truly deserve the title of "other masters" of American photography.

T. S. Bronson was a medical doctor in New Haven, Connecticut. The only son of wealthy parents, Bronson became interested in photography while in medical school. By the time he was thirty years old, he owned more than forty cameras. Although his success in medicine seemed assured, Bronson found himself spending more time with the camera than the stethoscope. By the age of forty he had taken more than forty-five thousand photographs. Finally he admitted his fate. He gave up his medical practice completely and devoted his life to turning his photography into art.

Like many other great photographers, Bronson was a perfectionist. He would set up his tripod and camera at a certain spot and spend the entire day taking shot after shot of the same scene until he captured it to his satisfaction. Bronson never opened a studio and, as far as we know, never sold his photographs for profit. He was interested in photography for photography's sake, and his subject was the newly arising American middle class. He photographed them at work, at play, and on the move.

In 1908 he photographed a scene at Lighthouse Point Beach in New Haven, Connecticut. His "Ladies on the Beach" (page 182) exemplifies his artistry. One can only imagine how long he

T. S. Bronson
Ladies on the Beach
1908

T. S. Bronson
A Sunday Stroll
1908

184

waited until the scene before him was exactly as he wanted it. But he snapped his shutter just as the woman at the right of the picture held her dark parasol in such a way as to balance the light parasol held by the reclining figure at the left. The flow of the garments, the faces of the two women in the center looking in opposite directions, the figure of the derby-clad man in the background, the cohesiveness of the whole group all combine to make "Ladies on the Beach" an outstanding photographic composition.

Working mainly with four-by-five and five-by-seven cameras, Bronson captured scores of memorable scenes of this new middle class. He had the ability to draw the viewer into his photographs, and in a picture such as "A Sunday Stroll" (page 183) one feels part of the group walking casually down a rural Connecticut road. And as is the case with many memorable photographs, the viewer is left with a sense of the mysterious. Who are these people? Where have they been? Where are they headed?

It was not until 1977 that Bronson's artistry gained national attention. Critics hailed his work as that of a "true photographic genius." T. S. Bronson is typical of all the artists in this section— a photographer whose acclaim has been long overdue.

While T. S. Bronson was using his photographic ability to record the lives of America's new white middle class, another photographer was training his camera on a totally different segment of the American population. James Van Der Zee, a black photographer, spent the better part of his life taking portraits and recording scenes of Afro-American life in Harlem, New York. Like T. S. Bronson, he approached photography as an art rather than

T. S. Bronson
The Couple
1906

James Van Der Zee
Cousin Susie Porter
1915

a craft. At the time Van Der Zee took his photographs, Harlem was the cultural capital of black America. Most of the black celebrities who either lived in Harlem or visited that community stopped at Van Der Zee's studio to have their portraits taken. All of Van Der Zee's portraits reveal a masterful command of composition, detail, and lighting. His photograph of his cousin entitled "Cousin Susie Porter," for example, is a sensitive and beautifully composed study.

Van Der Zee took many character studies that captured particular moods or unusual situations. His photograph of Rabbi Matthews and his congregation of black Moorish Jews, for instance, is memorable both as a group portrait and as a revelation of a way of life that relatively few Americans today realize ever existed.

Much the same can be said of his mood photographs. Pictures such as the one of the fur-clad couple, posed with their elegant automobile (page 189), reveal the existence of an affluent black society of which few outside this society were aware. It is a striking photograph, typical of Van Der Zee's attention to composition and detail.

Van Der Zee used his camera to record almost every aspect of life in Harlem—rallies, parades, street scenes, interiors, and organizations and groups of all kinds. Like T. S. Bronson, Van Der Zee was a true photographic master whose acclaim has been long overdue. In 1967, a young photographer named Reginald McGee "rediscovered" Van Der Zee's glass negatives, while conducting photographic research for the Metropolitan Museum of Art's

James Van Der Zee
Moorish Jews
c. 1910

James Van Der Zee
Couple with Car
1932

exhibition "Harlem on My Mind." The nation was then given the opportunity to recognize another previously little known master of American photography.

American women have played an important role in the history of photography. In recent years the work of two female photographers has begun to receive the attention it has long deserved. One of these women was named Chansonetta Stanley Emmons, and she was a member of a remarkable family. Chansonetta was the only daughter among six children. Two of her brothers, the twins F. E. and F. O. Stanley, were the developers of a dry-plate photographic process. Their dry plates became the most commonly used in all of turn-of-the-century America. Later the Stanleys became even more famous with their invention of the Stanley Steamer automobile.

The Stanleys lived in Kingfield, Maine, close to the Canadian border. In 1900 the entire population of the village numbered no more than eight hundred. It was in this setting that Chansonetta Emmons produced the remarkable photographs that have, at long last, gained her recognition as a master American photographer.

Chansonetta Emmons had a particular genius for posing her subjects in such a way as to produce photographs that were completely natural. Much of this had to do with the fact that she and her subjects were longtime friends and neighbors; but much of it was the result of her inborn sense of composition and of the dramatic.

What marked her work most vividly, however, was the way in which she used light in her photographs. As a recent biographer has said, "She used natural light exclusively, even for interior shots, and was able to employ it in a sculptural manner to create forms and spaces, allowing it to flow over and through the objects she placed in its path. The result was that reality was enhanced and improved, as it has been for centuries by artists of note."

This special ability with lighting is evident in such photographs as "Shelling Corn" and "Old Table Chair No. 2" (pages 192 and 193). One cannot look at these photographs without being struck by the magnificent way in which Miss Emmons used natural light to give a distinctive effect to her images. In "Shelling Corn" the light pouring through the window falls on the figures in such a way as to remind one of a Rembrandt painting. In "Old Table Chair No. 2" the light casts shadows on the wall that serve as a soft background to the sharp, sturdy features of the man in the chair.

For more than fifty years the young people of Kingfield, Maine, and the surrounding areas had been leaving the used-up farms. By the end of the nineteenth century almost no one was left on these farms but the old people. Along with her character studies, Chansonetta took photographs of farmers at work at 5:00 A.M. and of the women whose work never seemed to end. Thanks to her, a way of life that was quietly vanishing was captured forever in haunting and unforgettable photographs.

Another woman photographer whose work has recently come to be recognized as that of a true master was Alice Austen. Whereas Chansonetta Emmons used her camera to record life in a poor rural setting, the wellborn Miss Austen took photograph after photograph of Victorian social life on Staten Island and at Lake

Chansonetta Emmons
Old Table Chair No. 2
c. 1901

Chansonetta Emmons
Shelling Corn
1901

Chansonetta Emmons
Aunt Abigail Vose and Three Daughters
1898

Mahopac, New York. Like those of the Byrons, most of her photographs chronicle the parties, the sporting events, and the comings and goings of America's most privileged class. They show groups posed with tennis rackets, men and women on horseback following the hounds, people strolling through lovely formal gardens and parks.

But there was another side to Alice Austen. Like Frances Benjamin Johnston, Alice Austen was not content to photograph only the rich at their play. She took her camera on daylong excursions into New York City, where she took powerful photographs of people at work at occupations of every kind. One of her favorite haunts was the New York City waterfront. At the turn of the century it was alive with activity. Sailing and steam vessels of every description loaded and unloaded goods. Ships arrived daily from every port of the world. Miss Austen had an eye for capturing contrasts in her waterfront photographs. In one of her most dramatic pictures, sailing vessels and their unloaded cargo are seen at a dock at New York's famous South Street Pier (page 196). The viewer's eye is taken immediately with the huge, powerful ships and the heavy lumber and casks along the dock. But as one looks more closely at the picture, one suddenly notices the dandy swaggering along under his bowler hat in the foreground. He seems out of place in this scene of toil and power. Yet it is no accident that Miss Austen has caught and recorded his presence. It was this sense of irony that lent such interest to her pictures and set her apart from other photographers who may have had equal technical skill.

Alice Austen
Sailing Ships—South Street
c. 1885

196

While photographers such as Chansonetta Emmons and Alice Austen were preserving scenes of people and activities in the eastern part of the United States, half a continent away a Wisconsin photographer named Henry Hamilton Bennett was using his camera to capture landscapes and people at leisure in an area known as the Wisconsin Dells. This district, made up of small islands and gorges on the Wisconsin River, was a popular vacation spot for people in the Milwaukee region.

Actually, Bennett had a great deal to do with the Wisconsin Dells' becoming a well-visited recreation area. He was fascinated by the landscape of the region, and he spent more than thirty years photographing every nook and cranny of the Dells. Many of the people who came there did so having been lured by one of Bennett's photographs.

H. H. Bennett owned a very prosperous portrait studio, but he left that side of the work to his wife. His particular talent was for outdoor photography. He took marvelous photographs of locations within the Dells with such intriguing names as Skylight Cave, Steamboat Rock, Chimney Rock, and Boat Cave. Like some of the earlier photographers of the West, Bennett had a particular ability to capture the interplay between water, rock, sunlight, and shadow. He "framed" many of his subjects as they were about to enter the cavern by canoe. Thus, the natural rock served as a keyhole though which the viewer could gaze at the scene outside. H. H. Bennett photographed in a very special and exotic setting. But it was his own particular talent that allowed him to capture images that remain fixed in the memory of all who view them.

H. H. Bennett
Steamboat Rock
1903

H. H. Bennett
Skylight Cave
1903

American photographers, both amateur and professional, have always come from all walks of life. William Lyman Underwood, for example, was well known for his pioneering work in science. His family owned one of the largest food-canning companies in America. What has been little known until very recently, however, was that Underwood was also a dedicated photographer whose inventiveness, love of nature, and photographic skill enabled him to produce images that, like those of H. H. Bennett, can be called unique.

Only a few of Underwood's pictures were published while he was alive, and his achievements with the camera were largely forgotten until a collection of his photographs was rediscovered in 1977. What the collection and the logbooks that accompany it reveal is the work of a man seeking perfection in his photography. Once Underwood spent weeks working on a special photographic rig, which was installed in his canoe and used for taking nighttime photographs of animals. He was a man of unlimited patience and this trait obviously contributed to his particular ability to photograph wildlife. He took many scenes of the Maine woods, of his native Belmont, Massachusetts, and of exotic regions far from New England: streets and levees in New Orleans, the Florida Keys, villages in the Bahamas.

But it was nature in general and the wilderness and wildlife in particular that fascinated Underwood most and that served as the subject for many of his photographs. Using the special rig, he was able to capture an extraordinary nighttime picture of a deer standing at the edge of a pond. It is a typical Underwood photograph—

William Lyman Underwood
The Deer
1906

William Lyman Underwood
Children
1906

simple, direct, and striking. His other studies of owls, bears, and birds of all kinds are just as striking and reflect both his love of nature and his mastery with a camera.

It is not surprising that a man in love with the natural would also be fascinated by children. That this was so is evidenced by the scores of marvelous photographic studies he made of children in various settings. One photograph in particular, that of a young boy and girl standing knee-deep in the sea, seems to encapsulate all of the qualities of an Underwood photograph—directness, simplicity, honesty, and beauty.

As we have seen, the works of several of the photographers in this section might well have gone unnoticed forever were it not for discoveries made in very recent times. This is also the case with the photographs of Ulrich Bourgeois. It was only the chance discovery of a large collection of his glass negatives in a New Hampshire barn that led to an intensive search, which has uncovered scores of other Bourgeois photographs as well as a record of his life and those of many of his subjects, particularly Charles Lambert—the Hermit of Mosquito Pond.

Born in Canada, Bourgeois moved in the late 1800s to the textile manufacturing city of Manchester, New Hampshire. While working at various jobs, he became interested in photography and demonstrated such an obvious ability that he was hired to head the photographic department of one of Manchester's leading specialty stores. Like William Underwood, Bourgeois had an innovative mind. He was, for example, one of the first to perfect the technique of enlarging photographs to mural size. He was a man with a rich sense of humor, and it is reflected in many of his photographs.

His most striking work, however, revolved around one particular subject—the hermit Charles Lambert. Bourgeois was fascinated with the old man, who was already a legend in Manchester. Charles Lambert had been born in England. He had traveled the continent and spoke five languages. According to newspaper accounts of the 1880s, he had come to America and fallen in love with a woman who later jilted him. He then bought some land along Mosquito Pond in Manchester and spent the rest of his long life raising vegetables and herbs and living the life of a hermit.

Bourgeois became fascinated by the recluse. Through many visits and a great deal of patience he won his confidence and friendship. Eventually, Lambert allowed Bourgeois to do a photographic study of him—in his garden, at his traps, and in his ramshackle home. The annals of American history are filled with stories of hermits who lived in practically every area of the country. But no more dramatic or haunting photographic study has ever been done of such an individual than that conducted by Ulrich Bourgeois. His photographs of the Hermit of Mosquito Pond reflect the long hours he spent at his task and the talent he had for capturing the very essence of a human being through the camera. Bourgeois's particular skill with lighting effects and his patience in waiting for just the right expression and mood were rewarded with a magnificent series of photographs, remarkable for the insight they give us into the character and personality of an extraordinary individual.

Ulrich Bourgeois
The Hermit
c. 1895

Ulrich Bourgeois
The Hermit
c. 1895

Ulrich Bourgeois
The Hermit
c. 1895

The photographers discussed in this section are only a sampling of "other masters" of photography. There were many other turn-of-the-century artists, including Charles H. Currier, L. W. Halbe, George and Alvah Howes, and William Hester. There is no doubt that someday all of these and countless other pioneering camera-men and -women will take their rightful place in the annals of American photography.

In order to indicate, however, the scope and artistry of hitherto relatively unacclaimed turn-of-the-century photographers, this section concludes, not with the works of one photographer, but rather with a selection from an American photographic company. The Detroit Publishing Company was formed in 1898 by two men, William A. Livingston and William Henry Jackson. Livingston owned a company that held the American rights to a new Swiss process whereby one could successfully color black-and-white photoprints and lithographs. Jackson, as described earlier, was one of America's most important frontier photographers. The Detroit Publishing Company sent cameramen throughout the United States to make a turn-of-the-century photographic record of American cities and towns. Jackson himself took many of the photographs. A brilliant Boston photographer named Henry Peabody took thousands of others. The names of countless others in the company's employ are, unfortunately, lost forever.

The photographs that these cameramen and -women took are truly outstanding. They present an authentic visual documentation of life in every section of America at the turn of the century. Just as important, picture after picture reveals the work of a

Detroit Publishing Company
Biloxi, Mississippi
1906

genuine master of photography. There is a consistency of composition, detail, and artistry that makes the collection unique in photographic history. For example, a scene captured on the beach at Seabreeze, Florida, gives us a marvelous view of a vanished America. There are the ladies with their layers of long clothing. There are the horses and buggies. And if one looks closely, there is the earliest of automobiles. It is a wonderful visual document of the past, but it is also much more. The photographer has frozen the scene at the precise moment when individuals gazing to the left are balanced by individuals looking off to the right. And the photographer has picked out a section of the beach where the contrast between lights and darks in clothing, in vehicles, in the sand, and in the water all combine to produce an exceptional photograph.

These examples of artistic ability with a camera are present in photograph after photograph in the tens of thousands of pictures that make up the Detroit Publishing Company collection.

It is not the number of photographic prints but the consistent quality of the work that gives us concrete evidence that at the turn of the century masterful photographers operated throughout the United States. Their work serves as a perfect example of the way in which technical advances in cameras, plates, and other photographic equipment made possible the gathering of a magnificent record of life in every area of the United States—a record captured by "other masters" of photography.

Detroit Publishing Company
Seabreeze, Florida
1904

Detroit Publishing Company
South Boston
1906

Detroit Publishing Company
Providence, Rhode Island
1906

Detroit Publishing Company
Chicago
1905

Seven

Later Documentary Photography

The F.S.A.

THE YEAR WAS 1935 and the United States was in the midst of the greatest economic depression in its history. Businesses throughout the country were failing, and millions of people were unemployed. American farmers, who had always been regarded as the backbone of the United States, were particularly hard hit. In fact, thousands of farmers in the early 1930s were driven from their land by falling prices and record droughts.

In Washington, President Franklin D. Roosevelt took many actions in an attempt to end the depression and bring relief to the nation. One of his acts led to the formation of an agency called the Farm Security Administration, better known as the F.S.A. President Roosevelt and his advisers were determined that through the F.S.A. they would bring financial relief and give technical aid to American farmers. What no one could have dreamed was that one section of that agency—the Historical Section—would produce a photographic collection that would turn out to be the greatest ever assembled in the history of the United States.

The Historical Section of the F.S.A. was made up of a team of thirteen of the nation's top photographers. They were directed by a man named Roy Stryker. One of the purposes in forming this team was simply to provide employment for American photographic artists. Other important painters and photographers had already been put to work on other federal projects. Berenice Abbott, for example, took her marvelous pictures of New York City while working for the Federal Art Project. The most important aim, however, of putting together the F.S.A. photographic team was that of producing a pictorial record of rural America. As Stryker himself has said, "We introduced Americans to America."

Roy Stryker proved to be the perfect choice as director of the F.S.A. photographic project. From the beginning, he made it clear to all the photographers that their goal was not to chronicle a people caught up in the middle of agonizing economic times, but rather to record the dignity of the human spirit as it labored against adversity. His selection of photographers to accomplish this goal was superb. The F.S.A. team included such major American photographers as Walker Evans, Ben Shahn, Carl Mydans, Dorothea Lange, Arthur Rothstein, Marion Post Wolcott, John Vachon, Jack Delano, Russell Lee, and Gordon Parks.

Many of these photographers became famous through the work

Walker Evans
Country Store (Alabama)
1936 (F.S.A.)

Walker Evans
Bethlehem, Pennsylvania
c. 1935 (F.S.A.)

they did for the F.S.A. Walker Evans, for example, was already a well-known and respected photographic talent when he joined the team. But the pictures he took for the F.S.A. secured his place in photographic history. Evans had a style that was distinctly his own. He preferred everyday articles of life as his subjects, rather than people. He was able to photograph them in such a way that the simplest of these articles tell us much about the people who lived with and used them. In the words of one critic, Evans was the "world's greatest expert at photographing empty rooms in houses and making them echo with the people who lived there."

Symbols also played an important role in Evans's pictures. In a scene he photographed in Bethlehem, Pennsylvania (page 219), a huge cross in front of workers' homes and the steel mills offers a powerful commentary on the hard life of these people. The telephone poles also form crosses, accentuating those in the cemetery.

Evans's photograph of the washroom and kitchen of a cabin in Hale County, Alabama, is representative of many others he took. A plain basin, a hurricane lamp, a towel, a table and chair, a pitcher, and a simple cupboard—uncluttered everyday things that tell us much about the people who lived in the house.

While Walker Evans took photographs that, for the most part, avoided the inclusion of people, Dorothea Lange took a totally opposite approach. Her work focused almost entirely on people. She was particularly taken with the plight of those farmers who had been driven from their farms in the Southwest and who had been forced to the road in search of jobs in California. One need only look at the eyes and the hands of the people in her photographs to understand the desperate condition in which they had been placed.

One cannot look at Lange's photographs without becoming convinced that she had a real compassion and respect for the people who were her subjects. Her pictures captured the soul of the entire nation and inspired John Steinbeck's great novel *The Grapes of Wrath*. They eventually earned for Dorothea Lange a reputation as a documentary photographer equal to that of predecessors such as Jacob Riis and Lewis Hine.

The F.S.A. photographers produced more than 270,000 photo-

Walker Evans
Kitchen (Alabama)
1936 (F.S.A.)

Dorothea Lange
Migrants (California)
1936 (F.S.A.)

Dorothea Lange
Mother and Child (California)
1939 (F.S.A.)

Arthur Rothstein
Dust Storm (Oklahoma)
1936 (F.S.A.)

graphs. Probably the single most famous picture in the entire collection is that taken by Arthur Rothstein of a farmer and his sons caught in a dust storm. It is a masterpiece that has become one of the most well-known photographs of all time, a classic visual statement of man's battle against nature at its harshest. At the time it was taken it became a focal point in the movement for national soil conservation. Like so many other F.S.A. photographs,

Dorothea Lange
Greek Migratory Woman (California)
1936

Jack Delano
Laughter in a Tobacco Shed (Connecticut)
1940

it was a visual document that helped bring about needed reform.

Given the economic situation, many of the F.S.A. pictures portray people caught in the most difficult of times. The photographs of the children were particularly filled with pathos. But the photographers' respect for their subjects shows through in every

Russell Lee
After the Fourth of July Parade (Oregon)
1941

picture. In the entire F.S.A. collection there does not seem to be one photograph that gives evidence of a photographer's attempting to capture a subject in a degrading or condescending manner.

Some of the pictures are timeless. Russell Lee's photograph of an Oregon couple resting under a tree (page 227) is a warm, human, universal image that could have been taken anytime, anywhere. Most important of all, picture after picture exemplifies the major theme of the project: the unquenchable spirit of the American people. Perhaps Roy Stryker summed it all up best when he stated: "Dignity versus despair . . . I believe that dignity wins out." The F.S.A. project was completed in 1943. The photographs are now housed in the Library of Congress—a testimony to the spirit of the American people and the tremendous impact of the camera as a documentary device.

The O.E.O.

The 1960s were years of great social and political turmoil and unrest in the United States. America's long participation in the frustrating Vietnam War caused great divisions within the nation. Meanwhile, demonstrations, protests, and bitter arguments became almost commonplace as millions of Americans, particularly members of minority groups, sought to overcome the frustration of years of denial in gaining equal rights and opportunities.

In the midst of all of this turmoil, an important act was passed by the United States Congress. It was called the Economic Opportunity Act and was the vanguard of President Lyndon B. Johnson's Great Society program. What Americans were becoming increasingly aware of in the 1960s was that within a nation that boasted the highest standard of living in all the world, there were millions of people who were so poor that they could not afford adequate food, housing, clothing, medical care, or educational opportunities. The basic goal of the Economic Opportunity Act was to combat these problems and to "eliminate the paradox of poverty in the midst of plenty."

At the heart of the act was the formation of the Office of Economic Opportunity. The O.E.O., as it was called, was "to be a laboratory to devise programs to help the poor help themselves." Hundreds of self-help programs were funded and administrated by the O.E.O. Thousands of Americans of all ages worked on projects that brought aid to blacks, Mexican-Americans, American Indians, the young, the elderly, and the rural and urban poor.

O.E.O. agencies such as VISTA (Volunteers in Service to America), the Job Corps, and Project Headstart became well known throughout America. Other O.E.O.-funded agencies helped establish day-care centers, and created projects that, for example, helped Indians and Mexican-Americans build their own homes and establish their own medical and day-care centers. Still other O.E.O. organizations provided legal services of all kinds, set up craft programs, helped form farm and fishing cooperatives, established job colleges for minority students, and created much-needed drug and alcohol rehabilitation centers.

Like the F.S.A., which had come some thirty years before it, the O.E.O. hired a team of photographers to make a record of the people who were being helped and the progress that was being

Paul Conklin
Young Woman (Appalachia)
c. 1965 (O.E.O.)

Arthur Tress
Couple (Appalachia)
c. 1965 (O.E.O.)

232

made. As was the case with the F.S.A. photographic project, the goal of the O.E.O. cameramen and -women was to bring help to the nation's poor by making the whole country aware of the "paradox of poverty in the midst of plenty." And as was the case with the F.S.A., the photographic aspect of the O.E.O. produced a result of such high quality that it could never have been dreamed of by its founders and administrators.

The photographers hired by the O.E.O. were some of the most talented in the nation. Included in their ranks were Marcia Keegan, Paul Conklin, Martin Broffman, Arthur Tress, Day Walters, William Warren, Mark Sullivan, Linda Bartlett, and dozens of other outstanding contemporary photographers. They took their cameras into every part of the country to record living conditions among the disadvantaged and the ways in which the O.E.O. was working to "help the poor help themselves."

As one looks through the pictures in the O.E.O. collection, one cannot help being struck by how similar many of these images, taken in the 1960s, are to those taken by the F.S.A. documentary photographers in the 1930s. For example, in 1939 Russell Lee captured a dramatic image of a child peering out a window (page 234). Some thirty years later O.E.O. photographer Paul Conklin took an equally striking photograph of another youngster looking out a window (page 235). As one looks at these pictures and studies the expressions on the children's faces, one is struck by the timelessness of human need.

Some of the other parallels are equally heartrending. The documentary camera trained on people during hard times in both the

Russell Lee
Child (Oklahoma)
1939 (F.S.A.)

Paul Conklin
Child (Oklahoma)
c. 1965 (O.E.O.)

Arthur Rothstein
Mother and Child (Indiana)
1938 (F.S.A.)

Arthur Tress
Mother with Children (Illinois)
c. 1965 (O.E.O.)

Marcia Keegan
Woman (New York City)
c. 1965 (O.E.O.)

1930s and the 1960s picks up the universality of human suffering. This can be seen particularly in those photographs that show the anxious faces of mothers as they pose with their children.

As one studies the O.E.O pictures, it is obvious that the people who took them went about their task with the same sense of dedication as did the F.S.A. photographers. It is obvious too that the O.E.O. pictures were taken by photographers with great sensi-

Morton R. Engelberg
Boys on Corner
c. 1965 (O.E.O.)

Don Kimelman
Young Woman (Washington, D.C.)
c. 1965 (O.E.O.)

Paul Conklin
Indian (New Mexico)
c. 1965 (O.E.O.)

Morton R. Engelberg
Man (Baltimore, Maryland)
c. 1965 (O.E.O.)

tivity and skill. Perhaps this is because those in charge at the O.E.O. gave their photographers great freedom in their assignments. For example, speaking of one talented young photographer who was assigned to VISTA, an O.E.O. official stated: "The VISTA assignment propelled him all unready into new and unexpected situations. He had never done journalistic photography before, and tended to be too conscientious, taking the pictures he thought VISTA Magazine would want instead of the ones he wanted himself. Then he learned that the pictures he felt like taking were what VISTA really wanted, and the work became more rewarding."

Whatever the reasons, the photographs in the O.E.O. collection are powerful and important. They can stand on their own as dramatic documentary photographs taken by masterful photographers. More than words could, they show the paradox of poverty in the midst of plenty. But like the F.S.A. photographs, they show something more. In picture after picture, we are able to see the same remarkable quality that was brought out by the documentary photographers of the 1930s—the unquenchable ability of people to endure in the face of great adversity.

Eight

Color

"FROM THIS MOMENT FORTH painting is dead." These were the frantic words of the artist Paul Delaroche when he saw his first photograph. His fears were, of course, unfounded, and far from replacing painting, photography has joined it as another art form for the world to enjoy.

Within the world of photography itself similar fears were raised when, following World War II, a new type of color film was perfected, which enabled photographers to process their own color negatives and make their own color prints. For the first time the whole world of color was available to the camera's eye. But like those of Delaroche, the anxieties of the photographers who feared that color photography would replace black and white have proved to be unfounded. Instead, color has added a whole new dimension to photography. As Edward Weston said, "Those who say that color will eventually replace black and white are talking nonsense. The two do not compete with each other. They are different means to different ends."

Color photography is based upon the principle that any color can be re-created by mixing red, blue, and green light in varying proportions. In 1861 a British physicist, James Clerk Maxwell, superimposed these three colors on a screen and projected an image of a tartan ribbon. In 1868 a Frenchman named Louis Ducos du Hauron announced a process whereby color photographs could be produced on paper. This process was the basis for color photography until 1930, when Leopold Mannes and Leopold Godowsky, working with the staff of Eastman Kodak Company, developed the Kodachrome method of color photography. Through this method, it became possible to produce a positive color transparency on a single film that held three layers of emulsion, each sensitive to one of the colors. In 1938 both Kodachrome and a similar film, Agfacolor, became available to photographers everywhere.

Color photography has had a profound impact in many areas. It has changed the whole world of advertising. Through the use of color photographs, manufacturers can show their products to the public in the most realistic ways possible. For good or for bad, a talented photographer working in color can produce an image that is so appealing as to create a very real desire for the product on the part of the consumer. Today everything from a new type of cereal to the most luxurious automobile is first introduced to the public through color photographs.

Color photography has also had a pronounced impact on the

world of art, for it has made possible the reproduction of the world's great art treasures. Before color, art students had to content themselves with studying pictures of great paintings solely in black and white. Today color slides and prints make it possible to view the works of the master painters in full color no matter where the original paintings are housed.

The impact of color photography upon science is still in its infancy, but already new and exciting uses have been found. For instance, when infrared filters are used with color film, the world as we know it is changed dramatically. The photographs that result form a brilliant pattern of reds, yellows, browns, and blacks. Archaeologists use this process in seeking out buried sites. Military personnel use it to locate heavily camouflaged areas.

Color photography is used in medicine for many purposes. The exploration of outer space has been greatly enhanced by the availability of color film for use in the dramatic photographs taken on the moon, of Mars, and of the earth as seen from many thousands of miles away.

To the photographer, color presents a whole new world. By deliberately distorting images, by using certain colors to express human emotions, the photographer working in color can achieve results that were impossible less than fifty years ago. Talented artists such as Ernst Haas, Marie Cosindas, Gordon Parks, Nina Leen, Philippe Halsman, Larry Burrows, and Stan Wayman have used color to create masterful photographs. Their ingenuity and their understanding of the color process have enabled them to produce images that feature striking textures, designs, and pat-

Michael Zagaris
Dallas at San Francisco
1977

246

terns. Other photographers have used certain specific colors in their photographs as symbols for how they feel about the subject they are capturing on film.

With all its advantages, however, color also presents a challenge to the serious photographer. The temptation is great to use color itself as a means toward achieving a great picture. But, as is the case with black and white, it is not color but the photographer's

Unknown photographer
Advertisement
1977

Unknown photographer
Earthrise
1968

Ernst Haas
Park Avenue
1955

250

Ernst Haas
Nutcracker
1955

251

Eliot Porter
Aspens
1957

creative use of it that makes for a great photograph. Most fine color photographs, in fact, seem to be composed of subtle tones with carefully selected accents of bright color. Thus, a master photographer such as Eliot Porter is able to produce a beautiful nature study by combining the subtle tones of a stand of aspens with the brilliant golden accent provided by the leaves of an adjoining bush. Alfred Eisenstaedt creates an unforgettable portrait of a harbor by emphasizing subtle colors and soft tones.

Alfred Eisenstaedt
Mystic (Connecticut) Seaport
1970

Larry Burrows
Expo '70
1970

For amateur photographers, color is indeed the photographic medium of today. More than 80 percent of all snapshots are now taken with color film. For the millions who use the camera as an aid to preserving memories of people and events, color is an important ingredient in capturing forever the clothes one wore, the car one drove, or the look of a favorite spot on a particular day. Still, it is obvious that color photography will not replace black and white. In fact, relatively few of the world's great professional photographers use color as their main means of expression. Yet it is undeniably an important photographic form—another in a seemingly endless series of inventions and developments that make the art of photography always alive, always vibrant.

Nine

News Photography
and Photojournalism

News Photography

THROUGHOUT THE HISTORY of photography there have been many dramatic and far-reaching inventions. Unquestionably, one of the most important of these was the development of the *halftone plate* in the closing years of the nineteenth century. This invention made it economically possible for photographs to be printed in newspapers, books, and magazines, and led to two of today's most important photographic fields—news photography and photojournalism.

Photography had actually had an important influence on magazines and journals even before the invention of the halftone. Popular publication like *Harper's Weekly* and *Leslie's Magazine* hired photographers to take pictures of the leading personalities and events of the day. These photographs were converted into drawings and then into woodcuts from which the drawings could be printed in the magazines.

The reason that the photographs could not be printed directly was that the engraving and printing processes of the time could not reproduce a photograph alongside printing type on printing presses. This was because only the full tones of the photograph—the deep blacks and the stark whites—could be reproduced. The intermediate shades of gray so predominant in a photograph could not be reproduced.

This problem was finally solved with the invention of the halftone. The key to this process was the use of a screen of fine lines on glass that broke the photographic image into thousands of dots. The pattern of the dots was transferred photographically onto a chemically treated printing plate. All of the tones—blacks, whites, and grays—could be reproduced. Now photographs could be printed on the same press with type. Photographs could be reproduced in unlimited quantities in publications of all kinds. And all of this took place at the very time when other advancements such as dry plates, flexible film, and hand-held cameras were making the exposure of negatives easier than ever before.

There were, of course, cameramen and -women who could legitimately be called news photographers even before the invention of the halftone. Mathew B. Brady is a prime example. As we have seen, however, the slow wet-plate process, the bulky photographic equipment, and the lack of a means by which his Civil War photographs could be mass-produced in newspapers and magazines gave Brady only his own photographic galleries and the high-priced limited editions of his *Civil War Views* as a market for his work. One can only imagine what an impact Brady and his fellow Civil War photographers would have had in their own lifetimes if the halftone process had been available to them and if their photographs had been printed regularly in newspapers and magazines throughout America.

News photographers have always played a special role in photographic history. It is their job to seek out and take the most dramatic and timely photographs possible. The successful news photographer must have very special skills, including courage, patience, imagination, and the ability to produce photographs quickly enough to meet the ever-increasing pressures of newspaper and magazine deadlines.

Some of the scenes captured by news photographers will remain etched forever in the minds of the American people. These very special photographs have depicted every human emotion, every human experience. Through the news camera's lens we have been eyewitnesses to the most dramatic moments in modern history. We have seen Presidents inaugurated and world leaders assassinated. We have seen the miracle of birth and the anguish of death. We have witnessed natural phenomena such as hurricanes, blizzards, and drought, and such human-made marvels and catastrophes as man's ascent to the moon and the ravages of war.

Certain news photographs have struck the public with a particular kind of impact. During the Vietnam War, for example, a picture by news photographer Eddie Adams caused a tremendous

Eddie Adams
Execution in Saigon
1968

stir in nations around the world. Adams's camera captured a scene that shocked most of the people who viewed it, for it showed a South Vietnamese official with his pistol pointed at the head of an enemy soldier seconds before the official executed the soldier on the spot. The photograph was taken at a time when there were bitter divisions over America's participation in the war. The impact of the picture was such that emotions ran even higher. Like other great news photographs, it caused viewers to pause and reflect upon what they were seeing and the reasons for it.

Happily, not all news photographs are of tragedy or war. There are, for example, the dramatic and exciting sports photographs that appear daily in American newspapers. With interest in sports at an all-time high, it is a certainty that whenever a major sporting event takes place, a battery of news photographers will be there to capture the action.

News photographers were also there when, during the 1940s, a high-ranking business official refused to obey a court order to vacate his offices during a business-labor dispute. Millions of Americans chuckled at the picture of the determined executive who had been removed from his chair and carried out of the building by the two burly representatives of the law.

Because, in modern times, news photographers are nearly always present at every kind of newsworthy event, we have photographs of almost every conceivable happening. Sometimes the unexpected occurs, and if the news photographers are quick enough, they capture scenes that viewers will never forget. For example, in 1937 at the height of the era of dirigibles the great German airship *Hindenburg* was about to dock at an airfield in Lakehurst, New Jersey. The event drew a tremendous crowd of spectators, among them several news photographers. Just as the enormous ship was about to be secured, it exploded. Braving the intense heat and danger from the flames, several news photographers paused long enough before they fled for their lives to record the spectacular effects of the explosion (page 262).

More than any other form of photography, the impact of a news photograph often depends on the story behind the picture

Russ Russell
Touchdown
1977

Unknown photographer
Evicted
1944

261

Murray Becker
Hindenburg *Explosion*
1937

itself. For example, in 1948 President Harry S Truman was a decided underdog in his bid for reelection against Governor Thomas E. Dewey of New York. On the night of the election early returns seemed to indicate that Truman had indeed lost to his opponent. A major American newspaper was so sure of this that, in an attempt to "scoop" other papers, it printed an early edition with Truman's "defeat" proclaimed boldly across the front page. When all the votes were counted, however, Truman proved to be the winner by a narrow margin. The next day news photographers snapped the jubilant President as he delightedly displayed the newspaper carrying the false headline (page 264).

News photographs feature famous individuals and people whose names remain unknown to the public. What is important is that they make people aware of what is going on in the world and they convey all those feelings—courage, anguish, joy, sorrow—that are shared by humans everywhere. News photographers are always on the lookout for scenes that reveal humor, even under trying circumstances. Thus when, during the great blizzard of 1978, a young woman identified the location of her snow-buried car with a homemade sign, an alert news photographer was there to capture the moment (page 264).

The names of most news photographers are unknown to the general public. One exception, however, was a man named Arthur H. Fellig, who called himself "Weegee." He spent a great deal of time promoting himself and his work. On the back of each of his photographs he stamped the words "Credit Weegee the Famous." He was, however, an extremely talented news photographer who

W. Eugene Smith
False Headline
1948

Unknown photographer
Blizzard
1978

Weegee
Reaction to a Murder
1941

specialized in taking shots of violence in the streets of the city and the reaction of bystanders to this violence.

Today news photography is more popular and important than ever before. In an age when news events break so quickly that one can hardly keep up with them, in an age when television has raised the visual awareness of whole generations, the still news photograph is increasingly a major means of communication. Like all types of photography, it is raised to an art form when the person behind the camera has the skill and the sense of drama to freeze forever a moment that will remain indelibly etched in the mind of the viewer.

265

Photojournalism

"To see life, to see the world, to eyewitness great events; to watch the faces of the poor and the gestures of the proud; to see strange things—machines, armies, multitudes, shadows in the jungle and on the moon; to see man's work—his paintings, towers, and discoveries; to see things a thousand miles away, things hidden behind walls and within rooms, things dangerous to come to . . . to see and take pleasure in seeing; to see and be amazed; to see and be instructed."

It was with these words in 1936 that a purely photographic magazine was begun by Henry Luce, a man who was already the publisher of two other major American magazines, *Time* and *Fortune.* The new photographic magazine was called *Life,* and it was destined to play an important role in the history of American photography.

To see
and take
pleasure
in seeing

Alfred Eisenstaedt
Follow the Leader
1953

To see
and be
amazed

Robert Capa
Death of a Soldier
1936

To see
and be
instructed

WORLD'S HIGHEST STANDARD OF LIVING

There's no way
like the
American Way

Margaret Bourke-White
Contradiction
1937

267

Life was not the first magazine based on photographs. As early as 1890 a periodical known as *Illustrated American* made its appearance. With each succeeding issue, however, *Illustrated American* carried more and more captions until it was ultimately much more a journal than a photographic magazine. Other attempts were made to produce magazines based on photography, but they, too, went the way of *Illustrated American.*

It was with *Life* that the photographic magazine and photojournalism were truly established. It was the aim of its editors to replace the "haphazard" publishing of pictures with the "mind-guided camera." This theory of the mind-guided camera set *Life,* and later the publication *Look,* apart from all photographic magazines that had come before it. *Life's* stories were not hit-or-miss affairs. As one photographic historian has said, "They [were] planned and executed like military operations."

Life's picture essays involved both editors and photographers. Once a story was decided upon, a great deal of research was done into the subject and a "shooting script" was prepared well before the photographer went into the field. The purpose of the shooting script was to give the photographer as much of an understanding as possible of the mood, purposes, and content of the pictures needed. After the photographs were taken and developed, the editors chose those they felt best told the story. Then a layout of the selected pictures was prepared with blocks of space provided for words to be written by staff writers.

This carefully planned, mind-guided approach brought the necessary organization and structure to *Life's* photographic essays. What made many issues truly remarkable was the extraordinary talent of the photographers the magazine was able to hire. Alfred Eisenstaedt, for example, carried out more than fifteen hundred assignments for the magazine and produced some of the most dramatic photo essays ever taken. Eisenstaedt's ability to combine the dramatic with a fine sense of composition and detail resulted in scores of memorable *Life* photographs. His study of nurses posed along the stairwell of their dormitory reflects the

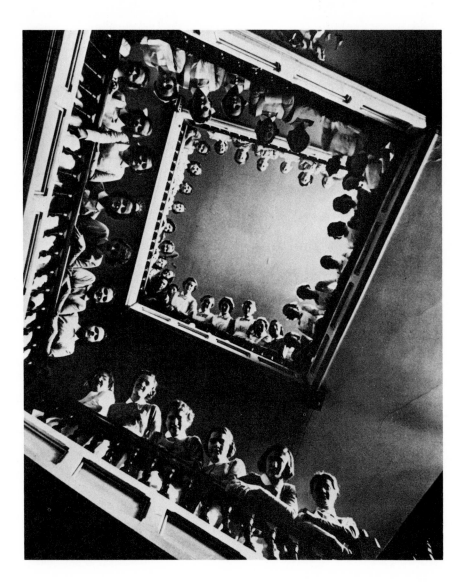

Alfred Eisenstaedt
Nurses
1937

Alfred Eisenstaedt
August 14, 1945
1945

270

work of a true artist with a camera. His picture of the sailor celebrating the news of the end of World War II was one of the best-known photographs of its time.

Margaret Bourke-White was another remarkable *Life* photographer. She was a photographer for *Fortune* magazine before Henry Luce assigned her to *Life*. Her picture of a giant dam in Montana was used as the cover for *Life*'s very first issue. Her work for *Fortune* and *Life* took her everywhere on the globe. It is estimated that she took more than a quarter of a million negatives. She was the only American photographer to record the Nazi bombing of Moscow in World War II. She was the first woman photographer assigned to the United States armed forces, and survived both the torpedoing of her troopship and the crash of a helicopter in which she was riding while doing a photo essay on United States Navy rescue techniques.

Her assignments took her to India, where her photographs captured the very soul of the Indian leader Mahatma Gandhi; to South Africa, where she descended deep into the earth to record black miners at work; to Germany, where in one photograph she captured the enormity of the tragedy suffered by millions of people in concentration camps such as Buchenwald. Her photographic essays covered industry, war, and foreign reporting. Her subjects included all of the world leaders of her time. As one critic has said, "Her work is a sort of candid eavesdropping, consciously controlled by the shape of the 35 mm. film she uses." As she herself said, "In some cases you feel you have stepped right into the lives of the people you are photographing."

Margaret Bourke-White
Mahatma Gandhi
1946

Margaret Bourke-White
South African Gold Miners
1950

Margaret Bourke-White
Buchenwald Victims
1945

273

Another photographic genius whose work appeared in *Life* through the years was W. Eugene Smith. Several of his photographic essays are among the most dramatic ever taken. His essay on a country doctor, for example, included photographs that not only revealed the work of a dedicated physician but cut through to the very heart of the man himself.

His essay on a Spanish village included an image of a woman spinning thread that is a true photographic masterpiece. As one

W. Eugene Smith
Country Doctor
1948

W. Eugene Smith
The Thread Maker
1951

studies Smith's photographs one can understand the words of Ansel Adams, who has said: "Gene Smith's work validates my most vigorous convictions that if the documentary photograph is to be truly effective it must contain elements of art, intensity, fine craft, and spirituality."

The roster of *Life's* photographers included many of the finest photographic artists of our time. George Silk, Ralph Crane, Nina Leen, and scores of others produced photo essays that were the very embodiment of the mind-guided camera. It is a sad commentary on human nature that the major events of the twentieth century have been dominated by wars, and in combat photography *Life* was without parallel. During World War II the magazine actually ran a school for army photographers. It was during this conflict and the Korean and Vietnam wars that major photographic talents such as Robert Capa, Chim (David Seymour), and David Douglas Duncan emerged. Their photo essays of the men and women whose lives were changed forever by these conflicts are among the most powerful ever taken.

Unfortunately, the serious economic problems that all magazines have faced through rising production and postage costs and the continuing competition for the public's attention in the form of television have caused many magazines either to shut down their presses or to publish much less frequently than before. *Look* is no longer published, and after ceasing operations for several years, *Life,* in 1978, began an attempt to establish itself again by publishing on a monthly rather than a weekly basis. But the place of these magazines in the annals of American photographic his-

Robert Capa
A Collaborator Escorted out of Town
1944

tory is secure, for they raised the photographic essay to a journalistic art form. They paved the way for a flood of photographic books, which in the last ten years have begun to add to the depth and scope of the photographic essay. As long as photographs are taken, the photographic essay will help us see the world in ways that words alone can never achieve.

David Douglas Duncan
Korea
1950

The World of Fashion

No discussion of photographs for the printed page would be complete without mention of the way in which newspapers and magazines, in the twentieth century, have come to rely upon photographs as a means of displaying and advertising the leading fashions of the day. As early as 1913, *Vogue* magazine began to feature fashion photographs. In the early 1920s Edward Steichen took many fashion pictures—in black and white and in color—that were published in both *Vogue* and *Vanity Fair*.

Since the 1940s the fashion field has relied heavily on photography. The list of fashion photographers includes some of the finest photographic talent in America. Gordon Parks, for example, has a well-earned reputation as a photojournalist. He is also a master of photo fashion. Another remarkable fashion photographer is Irving Penn, whose style is brilliantly distinctive, both in black and white and in color. Penn is a photographic explorer who has achieved unique effects in all areas of fashion photography. This is particularly interesting since Penn, unlike many other fashion photographers, uses almost no props and employs no trick or ornate lighting effects in his fashion photographs. The striking results he achieves come from his own ability to get at the heart of his subjects and to convey this to the viewer. Richard Avedon, another major modern fashion photographer, has taken a different approach. Many of his fashion photos are characterized by a feeling of motion. As one critic of Avedon's work has said, "His is a world of imagination. . . . His pictures have an unrehearsed and improvised, almost accidental air about them."

Whatever their approach, fashion photographers play an important role in the American photographic scene today. There is no question that through their special talents—the use of dramatic lighting, unconventional poses, and ever-changing techniques —they have strongly influenced the way people dress. Not incidentally, they have often provided us with striking and important photographic statements as well.

Irving Penn
*Girl in Black
and White*
1950

Béla Kalman
Untitled
1958

Ten

Photography for Today and Tomorrow

PHOTOGRAPHY is less than one hundred fifty years old, yet it is such a vital part of our life today that it is almost impossible to imagine our world without it. Pictures are everywhere. They fill the pages of our newspapers and magazines. They beckon to us from billboards, subway signs—even the boxes of the breakfast food we eat. The still photograph has become the most universal form of communication known to man.

The contributions made by photography to fields other than art would, in themselves, fill a volume larger than this one. Architects and builders, for instance, have long used photographic blueprints as the basis for their work. Scientists have placed cameras inside rockets and have used the resulting photographs to gain startling information about planets and stars. Meteorologists use photographs of cloud formations taken from earth-orbiting satellites to track dangerous storms. Photography has revolutionized

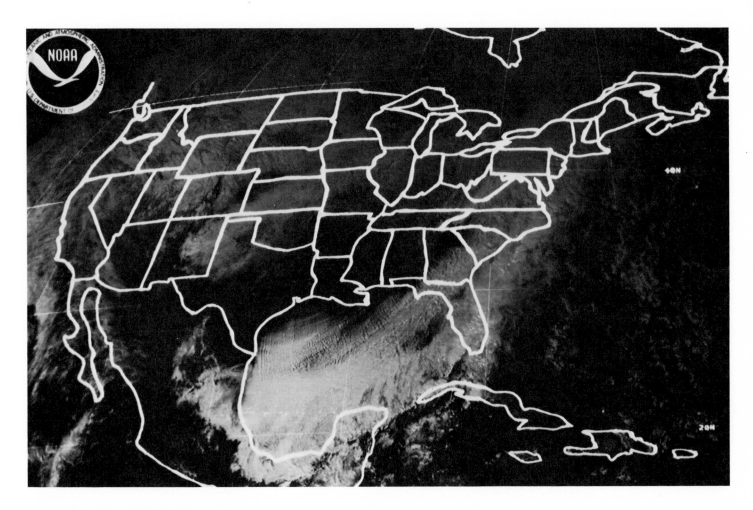

National Oceanic and Atmospheric Weather Satellite photograph
1978

283

the world of medicine. X-ray pictures allow doctors to probe every part of the human body in order to diagnose injuries and disease. Urban planners use aerial pictures to lay out city streets and plan shopping and recreational areas. Gas and oil companies use the pictures taken from the air to plot the course of their pipelines. The photographic process has become so advanced that it has changed the way countless products are made. This book, for example, was printed with photographically exposed plates. And, of course, the camera has changed completely the way products are sold. The still photograph is today the most important means by which goods are advertised to the public.

Photographs now allow us to see actions that are too fast for the naked eye to follow (a close play at first base). They allow us to see movement that is to slow for the naked eye (the various stages of the opening of a flower). Through the magic of the camera we see things too remote for our vision (the universe from outer space, the depth of the ocean floor). We study other things much too small for us to see on our own (bacteria and atoms). So advanced is photographic technology today that, as one photographic historian has put it, the average commercial photographer carries around his neck more equipment than Mathew B. Brady could have hauled in a caravan of his Whatsit wagons.

The photographic business has become a multibillion-dollar industry. There are, in fact, at least fifteen times as many camera shops as bookstores in this country, and they sell equipment more advanced and sophisticated than anything that could have been imagined even fifty years ago. The Polaroid-Land process, invented in 1947 by Edwin H. Land, for example, opened up a whole new photographic world, wherein the photographer not only takes the picture but receives the finished high-quality product on the spot within a matter of seconds. The single-lens reflex camera, light meters, high-speed film, special lenses—all are available to amateurs and professionals alike. No wonder that billions of photographs are taken every year in the United States alone.

Photography has led to the rise of two of the nation's most important industries—movies and television. Each of these fields grew out of the still photograph, and it is interesting to note how, increasingly, both of these mediums have begun to incorporate the still picture itself. The television industry, for example, is just beginning to realize the dramatic effect still pictures have on viewers when combined with the advanced technology of the television camera and the addition of music, narration, and sound effects.

There is no question that we live in a time when the photograph has became recognized as a legitimate art form. Museums everywhere now exhibit photographs alongside paintings and sculpture. Photographic exhibitions are held in galleries and museums throughout America and are enthusiastically attended. It is a most interesting fact that the fastest growing field within book publishing is that of photographic books.

With all these technical advances, with all this ever-increasing attention to photography, what about the men and women who use the camera as their means of livelihood today? It is always dangerous to put people and their work into neatly defined categories, but there do seem to be some definable trends in photography today. First of all, it seems clear that one can distinguish between those photographers whose work is done basically for themselves and those whose work is done for others. The first group we label "art photographers," while the others work chiefly for newspapers and magazines, advertising companies, government agencies, or corporations. Within both groups there are artists with special photographic talent. Another important distinction can be made, as well. In 1978 a major exhibition of contemporary American photography was held at New York's Museum of Modern Art. This exhibition was entitled "Mirrors and Windows." It distinguished between those modern photographers who approach their work as a means of self-expression and those who think of it as a method of exploration. Another way of expressing this might be to call these approaches romanticism in the first case and realism in the second. In the catalogue that accompanied this exhibition, John Szarkowski, the Museum of Modern Art's director of the Department of Photography, raised one of the most important questions that can be asked of a modern photograph: "Is it a mirror, reflecting a portrait of the artist who made it, or a window through which one might better know the world?" The final section of this book contains examples of both approaches to modern photography.

There is no question that the dean of modern photographers is Ansel Adams. He has earned this title, not only with the magnificent photographs he has taken, but through the photographic theories he has put forth and the scores of young photographers he has taught and whose work he has influenced profoundly. His

Ansel Adams
Moon and Half Dome
1966

Ansel Adams
Mount Williamson, California
1944

Ansel Adams
288

"Zone System of planned photography" has served as an important guide to modern photographers in achieving maximum impact in shooting, developing, and printing their photographs. Adams is a gifted pianist who gave up this career for photography in 1930. But the musician striving for precise technique is always apparent in his photographs. As he himself has said, pictures are "slight variations on a theme in photography."

For Adams, this photographic theme has always been nature—particularly the majestic landscapes of the Far West. He has photographed landscapes on the grandest scale. He is a realist in his approach. His uniqueness lies in the way he is able to use light and shadows and the way in which he composes his photographs, which often consist of foreground, mountain peaks, and sky. Endowed with unbounded energy, Adams has been able to present his work to a vast audience through countless major exhibitions and a great many books and portfolios of carefully reproduced examples of his work. In a career that has spanned more than half a century, Ansel Adams has maintained a consistency and quality that are an inspiration to artists everywhere.

Another very important and influential modern photographer was Minor White, a man who has sometimes been called "the poet with a camera." For White, the simplest object could be the basis for a photograph that expressed the strongest personal feelings. His goals, as he said, were "to photograph some things for what they are, and others for what else they are."

Through his photographs, his books, his exhibitions, and his teaching, Minor White has influenced scores of modern photogra-

Minor White
Capitol Reef, Utah
1962

phers. He was one of the founders of the photographic magazine *Aperture*. The importance of this publication cannot be overstated. It was instrumental in putting forth the idea of self-expression as an approach to modern photography. Its influence can be seen in the works of such important contemporary photographers as Paul Caponigro, Bruce Davidson, Walter Chappell, and Jerry N. Uelsmann, to name but a few.

Bruce Davidson
5 & 10¢ Store Lunch Counter
1963

Paul Caponigro
Blue Ridge Parkway
c. 1970

Paul Caponigro
Petrified Forest, Arizona
1975

Harry Callahan is another photographer who, like Minor White, has made the expression of his own inner feelings the basis for his photographs. His pictures actually can be separated into two categories. There are those that are very concrete—a mother and child, pedestrians frozen in front of modern city buildings. There are others that, by the use of such techniques as multi-exposure, are almost abstract. Callahan has been called "the photographer of the commonplace." This is because of the way in which he has attempted, through his photographs, to make even the most familiar things beautiful.

Harry Callahan
Chicago Loop
1952

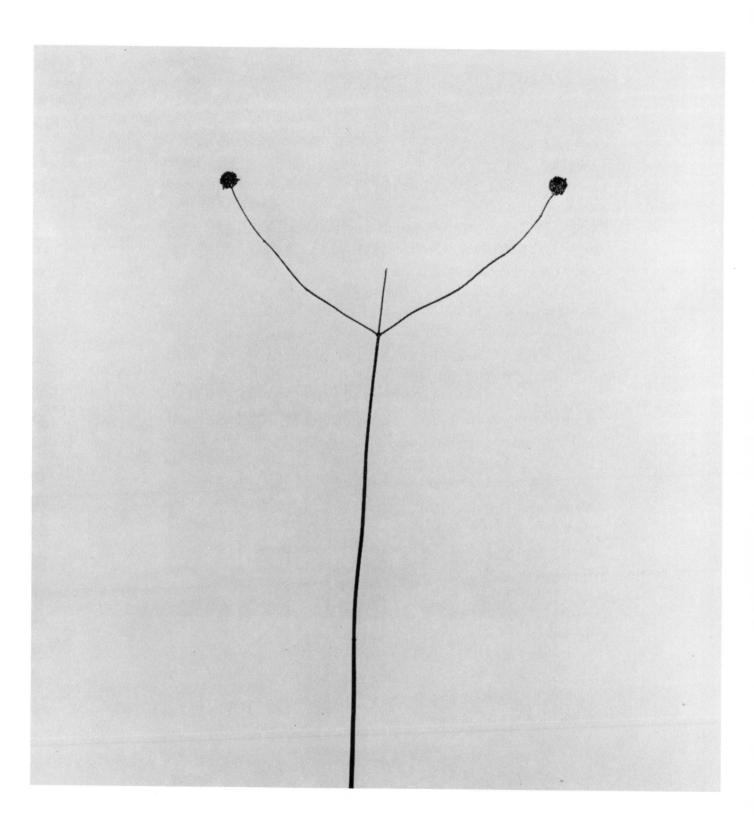

Harry Callahan
A Weed
1951

His technique is based upon simplicity. He concentrates on simple lines and simple patterns. By combining these with sharp contrast of dark tones and bright shades of white and adding his own personal interpretation to every picture he takes, Callahan has been able to create a remarkable photographic style. It is a style that many photographers have tried to imitate but that few have been able to equal.

Aaron Siskind is another modern photographer whose work has had a good deal of influence on scores of other cameramen and -women. Siskind began his career as a documentary photographer. His early work concentrated on such subjects as New York's Harlem and Bowery sections. But suddenly in the 1940s he did a complete about-face and took a totally different approach to his work. Instead of the starkly realistic pictures he had always taken, Siskind began to concentrate on abstract images. Particularly, he began to take close-up photographs of everyday objects that one usually ignores. He began to photograph walls, discarded pieces of metal, oil and water stains on paper. Speaking of this dramatic change in his style, he explained, "For the first time in my life, subject matter as such had ceased to be of primary importance."

For Siskind the photograph itself is far more important than the scene it depicts. It is not crucial to read a particular meaning into a Siskind photograph, but it is important to appreciate the design and structure of the picture itself, and the special, perhaps unstatable, meaning the photograph has for each individual viewer. Siskind speaks for scores of other photographers when he says, "I regard the photograph as a new object to be contemplated for its own meaning and its own beauty."

Aaron Siskind
Peeling Paint
1949

Aaron Siskind
Water Stains on Wallpaper
1949

Aaron Siskind is one of a large number of American photographers who use the camera in ways far removed from those of the traditional photographers of the past. Other photographic artists now use the medium to express every form of inner emotion. The work of the photographers who have broken all barriers of traditional photography is often startling. A prime example of this is the work of Arthur Tress. This young New Yorker first gained attention with a photographic exhibition sponsored by the Sierra Club and entitled "Open Space in the Inner City." The photographs he took for this exhibition led Tress to a study of those phenomena he remembered most from his childhood—dreams. He then began to interview scores of youngsters about their own dreams and to translate these dreams into photographs.

In 1972 Tress's book *The Dream Collector* was published. The startling photographs and accompanying text inspired a whole new look at the inner workings of children's minds—and a whole new approach to contemporary photography.

The photographs of Aaron Siskind, Arthur Tress, and others demonstrate graphically how talented photographers can explore any subject with depth and perception. Meanwhile, like Ansel Adams, there are countless other photographers working today who continue in the traditions of those who have come before them. Each, however, adds his own distinctive style to his work. Lee Friedlander, for example, is often regarded as the chief representative of today's school of documentary photography. Working with a 35-mm camera, he has produced powerful images of life in contemporary America. Friedlander's pictures have been

Arthur Tress
Dream (Loss of Identity)
c. 1970

Arthur Tress
Dream (Caught in Maze)
c. 1970

described as "unpretty." More accurately, in the tradition of all fine documentary photographers, they are real. He captures scenes of neon lights, bored people, television studios—photographs that reflect the cigarette smoke of the conference room and the noise of the city. Like many of today's documentary photographers, Friendlander has found books to be the best vehicle in which to put forth his portrayal of twentieth-century American life.

In this regard Friedlander follows in the tradition of an extremely important contemporary photographer, Robert Frank. Frank's book *The Americans* shocked people in this country when it was published in 1959, and it now stands as one of the most influential collections of documentary photographs taken in our time.

Frank's starkly realistic photographs focused on the gaudiness and hypocrisy in American culture. In much the same way that the work of Minor White and others published in *Aperture* influenced the photographers who saw their art as a means of self-expression, or what Alfred Stieglitz would have called "equivalents," Frank's *Americans* became a catalyst for cameramen and -women who saw their art as a means of exploration, or as realism. Included among the many important contemporary photographers who were strongly influenced by Frank are Garry Winogrand, Geoff Winningham, and Bill Owens.

One of the most extraordinary of all the modern photographers who have sought realism in their work was the late Diane Arbus. She took her camera into places where those more timid were afraid to go. She photographed people in mental hospitals, people

Lee Friedlander
Untitled
1966

Robert Frank
Political Rally
1956

Geoff Winningham
Friday Night at the Coliseum
1970

Diane Arbus
Untitled
c. 1970

with physical deformities, people in grotesque situations. Of her work, she said, "I really believe there are things which nobody would see unless I photographed them."

"Unless I photographed them." The photographers whose work we have examined in this section have, no matter what their approach, one basic thing in common—the passion to photograph. Through exhibitions, portfolios, and books they have received well-deserved critical acclaim.

In America today there are scores of talented, young, serious photographers who share this passion to photograph. Many of them will someday receive the widespread recognition they deserve. The concluding photographs in this book are illustrations of the work of three of these talented artists: Robin J. Brown, David Gengler, and Bernis von zur Muehlen. Of her photographs, Brown has said, "To me the unmanipulated photographic image can function simultaneously as a record of a place and time, and also as a symbol with life and meaning of its own." Gengler has stated, "My involvement with photography is emotional. Feelings are not well described with words. I take pictures to communicate, to express feelings." Von zur Muehlen has said, "I am interested not in recording what I perceive to be 'out there' but rather in uniting the internal with the external vision." Through their photographs and their words we can see the range of their abilities, the various approaches to the art of photography.

The art of photography! With all that has happened in the development of this amazing phenomenon—this combination of science and art—it is difficult to believe that photography itself

Robin J. Brown
Untitled
1976

David Gengler
Tree in Snowstorm
1976

Bernis von zur Muehlen
Brian McCall
1975

is less than one hundred fifty years old. With all of its technical advances, different approaches, and continuous innovations, what is it that best characterizes this newest of art forms? More than anything else, it is the knowledge that it is not the camera itself but the person behind the camera who, by bringing his or her own artistry, creativity, and sensitivity to the work, makes the difference in whether the end result is just another photograph or a true work of art.

From cave drawings to paintings, man has used a steady progression of vehicles for artistic expression. The photograph is the latest outlet for this creative spirit. Given how far it has come in so short a span of time, it is not surprising that there are those who state that photography will be *the* art of the twenty-first century.

Acknowledgments
and Picture Credits

It is with deep gratitude that I acknowledge the encouragement and aid I have received from John Wilmerding, assistant director of the National Gallery of Art; Daniel W. Jones, photoarchivist of the Peabody Museum of Harvard University; and John Keller, children's book editor of Little, Brown and Company. Special thanks go to Shirley Green, certainly the nation's outstanding photographic researcher, to Eva Nutt of *Life* magazine, and to Arthur D. Hynes. Appreciation is extended to historical societies, museums, and photographers who have allowed me to reproduce their photographs. Specific acknowledgment of each of these institutions and individuals is made below. Finally, this book would not have been possible without the efforts of two very special people. Melissa Clemence has edited this volume with skill and care that go well beyond the call of duty, and the dedication and craft with which Robert Lowe has designed it show through on every page. To them, the highest accolade — they are true professionals.

Sources of the photographs appearing in this book are as follows:

Courtesy of Ansel Adams: pages 287, 288–289
Courtesy of The Art Institute of Chicago: pages 107, 109, 110, 111, 112–113, 121, 122
Courtesy of Ed Bishop and Stop and Shop Companies, Inc.: page 248
Courtesy of Robin J. Brown and Panopticon Gallery: page 307

Suggestions for
Further Reading

Abbott, Berenice. *Berenice Abbott: Photographs*. New York: Horizon Press, 1970.

Adams, Ansel. *Ansel Adams: Images, 1923–1974*. Boston: New York Graphic Society, 1974.

Adams, Ansel. *Singular Images*. Boston: New York Graphic Society, 1974.

Aperture History of Photography Series. Millerton, N.Y.: Aperture, 1976.

Arbus, Diane. *Diane Arbus: An Aperture Monograph*. Millerton, N.Y.: Aperture, 1972.

The Art of Photography. Life Library of Photography. New York: Time-Life Books, 1971.

Auer, Michel. *The Illustrated History of the Camera*. Boston: New York Graphic Society, 1975.

Avedon, Richard. *Portraits*. New York: Farrar, Straus, 1976.

Beaton, Cecil, and Gail Buckland. *The Magic Image: The Genius of Photography from 1839 to the Present Day*. Boston: Little, Brown and Company, 1975.

The Best of Life. Morristown, N.J.: Silver Burdett, 1973.

Bisbee, A. *The History and Practice of Daguerreotyping*. Reprint of 1853 edition. New York: Arno, n.d.

Boesen, Victor, and Florence C. Graybill. *Edward S. Curtis: Photographer of the North American Indian*. New York: Dodd, Mead, 1977.

Brewster, David. *The Stereoscope, Its History, Theory and Construction*. Reprint of 1856 edition. Dobbs Ferry, N.Y.: Morgan and Morgan, 1971.

Capa, Cornell. *David Seymour*. New York: Viking Press, 1974.

Capa, Cornell. *Lewis W. Hine*. New York: Viking Press, 1974.

Capa, Cornell, ed. *The Concerned Photographer*. New York: Viking Press, 1972.

Caponigro, Paul. *Paul Caponigro: An Aperture Monograph*. Millerton, N.Y.: Aperture, 1972.

Color. Life Library of Photography. New York: Time-Life Books, 1970.

Craven, George M. *Object and Image: An Introduction to Photography*. New York: Prentice-Hall, 1975.

Curtis, Edward S. *The North American Indians*. Edited by Joseph E. Brown. Millerton, N.Y.: Aperture, 1972.

Documentary Photography. Life Library of Photography. New York: Time-Life Books, 1972.

Edson, Russell, and Peter C. Bunnell. *Jerry N. Uelsmann*. Millerton, N.Y.: Aperture, 1971.

Eisenstaedt, Alfred. *People*. New York: Viking Press, 1973.

Evans, Walker. *Photographs for the Farm Security Administration*. New York: Da Capo Press, 1974.

Frank, Robert. *The Americans*. Reprint of 1958 edition. Millerton, N.Y.: Aperture, 1978.

Friedman, Joseph S. *The History of Color Photography*. New York: Hastings House, 1968.

Fuller, et al. *The Instant It Happened*. New York: Abrams, 1976.

The Great Photographers. Life Library of Photography. New York: Time-Life Books, 1971.

Haas, Ernst. *The Creation*. New York: Penguin Books, 1976.

Hoffman, Michael E., and Minor White, eds. *W. Eugene Smith: His Photographs and Notes*. Millerton, N.Y.: Aperture, 1970.

Humphrey, S. D. *American Hand Book of the Daguerreotype*. Reprint of 1858 edition. New York: Arno, n.d.

Kunhardt, Dorothy Meserve, and Philip B. Kunhardt. *Mathew Brady and His World*. New York: Time-Life Books, 1977.

Meredith, Roy. *Mr. Lincoln's Camera Man: Mathew B. Brady*. New York: Dover Books, 1974.

Newhall, Beaumont. *The Daguerreotype in America*. Magnolia, Mass.: Peter Smith, 1976.

Newhall, Beaumont, and Diana Edkins. *William H. Jackson*. Dobbs Ferry, N.Y.: Morgan and Morgan, 1974.

Peladeau, Marius B. *Chansonetta: The Life and Photographs of Chansonetta Stanley Emmons*. Waldoboro, Maine: Maine Antique Digest, 1977.

Penn, Irving. *Worlds in a Small Room*. New York: Viking Press, 1974.

Porter, Eliot. *Portraits from Nature: A Portfolio*. New York: E. P. Dutton, 1973.

Rothstein, Arthur, et al. *A Vision Shared: The Words and Pictures of the FSA Photographers, 1935–1943*. New York: St. Martin's Press, 1976.

Sandler, Martin. *The Way We Lived: A Photographic Record of Work in a Vanished America*. Boston: Little, Brown and Company, 1977.

Steichen, Edward. *A Life in Photography*. Garden City, N.Y.: Doubleday, 1968.

Stryker, Roy E., and Nancy Wood. *In This Proud Land: America, 1935–1943, As Seen in the Farm Security Administration Photographs*. Boston: New York Graphic Society, 1973.

Szarkowski, John. *Looking at Photographs: One Hundred Pictures from the Collection of the Museum of Modern Art*. Boston: New York Graphic Society, 1973.

Szarkowski, John. *Mirrors and Windows: American Photography Since 1960*. New York: Museum of Modern Art, 1978.

Szarkowsky, John, ed. *From the Picture Press*. New York: Museum of Modern Art, 1973.

Thornton, Gene. *Masters of the Camera: Stieglitz, Steichen, and Their Successors*. New York: Holt, Rinehart, and Winston, 1976.

Tractenberg, Alan. *America and Lewis Hine*. Millerton, N.Y.: Aperture, 1977.

Tress, Arthur, and John Minahan. *The Dream Collector*. Richmond, Va.: Westover Publishing Company, 1972.

Weegee [Arthur Sellig]. *Weegee's People*. Reprint of 1946 edition. New York: Da Capo Press, 1975.

Weinstein, Robert A., and Larry Booth. *Collection, Use, and Care of Historical Photographs*. Nashville, Tenn.: American Association for State and Local History, 1977.

Weston, Edward. *Daybooks of Edward Weston*. 2 vols. Millerton, N.Y.: Aperture, 1973.

White, Minor, ed. *Octave of Prayer*. Millerton, N.Y.: Aperture, 1972.

Index

Page numbers in italics indicate photographs.